Reluctant Modernization

Andreas Hess

Reluctant Modernization

Plebeian Culture and Moral Economy in the Basque Country

PETER LANG
Oxford · Bern · Berlin · Bruxelles · Frankfurt am Main · New York · Wien

Bibliographic information published by Die Deutsche Bibliothek
Die Deutsche Bibliothek lists this publication in the Deutsche Nationalbibliografie; detailed bibliographic data is available on the Internet at <http://dnb.ddb.de>.

A catalogue record for this book is available from The British Library.

Library of Congress Cataloging-in-Publication Data:

Hess, Andreas.
Reluctant modernization : plebeian culture and moral economy in the Basque country / Andreas Hess.
p. cm.
Includes bibliographical references and index.
ISBN 978-3-03911-908-0 (alk. paper)
1. Basques--Ethnic identity. 2. Basques--Social conditions. 3. Basques--Economic conditions. 4. País Vasco (Spain)--Civilization. 5. País Vasco (Spain)--Social conditions. 6. País Vasco (Spain)--Economic conditions. 7. Pays Basque (France)--Civilization. 8. Pays Basque (France)--Social conditions. 9. Pays Basque (France)--Economic conditions. I. Title.
GN549.B3 H47 2009
306.099'992--dc22

2009008698

Cover image: Mutriku (Gipuzkoa), 1912
Cover design: Mette Bundgaard, Peter Lang Ltd

ISBN 978-3-03911-908-0

Printed in Germany

Contents

Acknowledgements

The initial idea of analysing aspects of moral economy in the peculiar context of the Basque Country came from Diana J. Holubowicz while I was conversing with her about the peculiarities of a fish auction in the Mutriku *cofradía*. I owe the greatest thanks to my friends from Mutriku, Gipuzkoa, Pello Andonegi and Idoia Arrizabalaga who made the idea more intelligible. Without their constant support and suggestions this book would not have emerged. I take this opportunity to extend my gratitude to the many other members of the Andonegi and Arrizabalaga families, and also to Fran Hermo and Nerea Larrañaga from Ondarroa, Bizkaia. I would particularly like to thank Joseba Zulaika for his continuous support and reading earlier drafts of the manuscript. A research grant from University College Dublin allowed me to employ a part-time researcher in the Basque Country. Anke van Wijck, who took on that job, provided help which went beyond all my expectations. She tracked down and copied relevant archival material, historical sources and numerous articles in the libraries of the Universities of Deusto, Bilbao and the two University of the Basque Country (UPV) campuses in Leioa and San Sebastián. Finally, I would like to express my thanks to Tom Garvin, Eldrid Herrington, Michael Laffan, Pello Lezertua, Ivar McGrath, Stephen Mennell, Ronnie G. Moore, Daragh O'Connell, Cormác O'Grada, John Sheehan and Paddy Woodworth who have either read the whole text or commented on previous drafts of individual chapters or have contributed in other ways to the completion of this book.

A version of the chapter on gastronomic societies appeared as 'The Social Bonds of Cooking: Gastronomic Societies in the Basque Country' in *Cultural Sociology*, Vol. 1, Number 3 (November 2007), 383–407.

The National University of Ireland supported the publication of this book with a grant under the NUI's Publications Scheme.

CHAPTER 1

Introduction: From the Critique of Basque Egalitarianism to an Understanding of Reluctant Modernization

> Conceivably, there are 'noble' and 'plebeian' nations, the first always a threat, the second always threatened.
> — MICHAEL WALZER 'Nation and Universe', Tanner Lectures 1990

In his groundbreaking study *El 'igualitarismo' vasco: mito y realidad* (1986) Alfonso de Otazu attempted to deconstruct the idea that since time immemorial a notion of egalitarianism has prevailed in the Basque Country. Against the idea that every Basque was a *hidalgo* – a nobleman – Otazu shows that some people were not only more noble or more equal than others but also that the very idea of equal and widespread noble origin usually served those in the ascendancy looking for power; at other times it helped those who were already in power in defending their privileged positions. Contrary to the idea that Basque society and culture were somehow less bound by class distinctions, and against nationalist tendencies to idealize a glorious past, Otazu describes the many historical layers of class conflict that arise when a country embarks on the long effort of transition and modernization from the Middle Ages to modern capitalism. In the Basque case, according to Otazu, that long transition can be studied in a number of historical constellations, starting with the transition from 'bandit country' to a more orderly and Castile-dominated *señorío* status, or even smaller administrative and economic units such as the *hermandades* (brotherhoods) and finally to the formation of the modern Basque provinces.[1] Particularly in times of transition we can, Otazu argues, encounter various forms of class struggle, often of a local dimension. Thus the conflicts in the Atlantic coastal regions of Bizkaia and Gipuzkoa took a very different form when compared to struggles in the interior of these provinces or in Alava or Navarre. The conflict between countryside and rural conditions versus the rising importance of an urban environment, including trade, commerce and industry, runs like a thread through Basque history and culture. Otazu refers to such events as the *revolución de sal* in Bilbao in the sixteenth century, the *matxinadas* of the early seventeenth century in Bizkaia and Gipuzkoa, or the selling of communal land towards the end of the eighteenth century and the powerful and hegemonic role that property, capital and educational qualifications played in it.[2] Yet, descriptions such as 'powerful' or 'hegemonic' do not necessarily entail 'secure' positions – hence the persistent appeal of the different oligarchies, either in the ascendant or already in power, to a common egalitarian inheritance. According to Otazu, the oligarchies' claims to property and access were usually supported by intellectual rationalizations from the clergy of religious orders. A strong Jesuit influence can easily be detected, most prominently in the case of Padre Larramendi, the first proto-nationalist to make the case for Basque egalitarianism. Later on, enlightenment circles such as the *Sociedad Vascongada* also became influential. On each occasion the minority in power or ascending to power used an appeal to the egalitarian collective memory to justify the inequalities that came with change, usually by evoking a sense of underlying accepted forms of an older equality that simply needed to be 're-adjusted' or to be 'brought up to date'.

1 The exception here is Navarre whose path overlapped and repeatedly crossed with that of the Basque provinces until the second half of the nineteenth century; it has since then followed a more independent political path, a route which was the cause of new lines of conflict such as the feeling of alienation of the northern Basque-speaking part of Navarre.

2 For a historical overview of these local disturbances and revolts see Porres Marijuan, R. (2004) 'El poder de los conflictos locales', in: Angula Morales, A. et al. (eds), *Historia del País Vasco – Edad Moderna*, San Sebastián: Hiria, 237–289.

Otazu should be commended for his groundbreaking study, particularly since it led to a number of important investigations that took seriously the issue of social inequality and class and how it related to modernization.[3] Yet, while showing that Basque society has always been subject to stratification (like any other region or nation) and that social stratification is not just something that is simply imposed by the outside world (i.e. Castile, the Spanish state),[4] two specific points were somehow obliterated. Firstly, Otazu and those historians and social scientists who accepted the logic of his argument looked only at the objective dimensions and the historically verifiable data and circumstances which supported their claim. The collective-subjective and moral dimensions of past and present conflicts disappeared and often fell off the social scientists' and historians' radar screen. Secondly, studying peculiar Basque motives and occurrences such as the obvious and easily identifiable appeal to the common good and the prevailing egalitarian and subjective sense of justice drifted somehow into the background or were forgotten.[5] In a new study, *El espíritu emprendedor*

3 Otazu was not the first one to discuss the relationship between nation and class. Amongst his predecessors Beltza (1976 and 1976a) and Carlos Nuñez (1977) stand out. These pioneering analyses, together with Otazu's study, were followed by many other studies of social stratification, now including the official analysis of the statistics bureau of the Basque government, Eustat.

4 This is not to deny links that existed and still exist between the Basque political and economic elite and the Spanish state or any of its other regions. However, it would be rather old-fashioned third-world Marxism or Leninism to anticipate that somehow a 'comprador bourgeoisie' existed that functioned as a lackey of the 'real' power (i.e. the Spanish capitalist elite) and that these links then explain all aspects of the conflict between Madrid and the Basque Country.

5 In this respect Jesús Arpal's study *La Sociedad Tradicional en el País Vasco* (1979) seems to me to be more balanced than Otazu's. While Arpal addresses also the question of inequality under pre-capitalist conditions in the Basque Country, he is less prone to argue that the rhetoric of egalitarianism is a mere device of the elite or ruling class. Arpal is also more inclined to look at how exactly family origin and family estates were reproduced and passed on, particularly in times when old and noble families were under pressure, either through some form of family reproduction crisis in the next generation, local pressures or external demands. Arpal is also more explicit than Otazu in showing that noble status did not express itself only through the wealth of

de los vascos (2008), which in many ways extends the argument first presented in *El 'igualitarismo' vasco*, Otazu and his fellow writer, Díaz de Durana, have taken the argument about the instrumental aspect of ideological egalitarianism even a step further. Now it is taken to have laid the foundations for the 'export' of the (male) Basque surplus population to the Kingdom of Castile and the Castilian colonial empire for the purpose of becoming successful 'spiritual' entrepreneurs in an almost Weberian sense. These Basque entrepreneurs are now shown to have replaced the old supply structure of the elite consisting mainly of Jews and/or *conversos*. While this is all described in fascinating detail, what remains problematic is the view of a 'trickle-down' effect of this new Basque egalitarian ideology and spirit. It is not by chance that the subject hero of the new study is the *emprendedor* (the entrepreneur) but almost never the Basque shepherd, peasant, artisan or fisherman. The latter are all at the receiving end of the modernization effort. This is heavy 'top-down' history writing – maybe contrary to the intent of the authors. The sources which have survived and on which Otazu and Díaz de Durana rely heavily stem mostly from those who knew how to write and to execute power. In contrast, the subaltern classes rarely expressed themselves in either written form, be it in government statutes or in official speeches and pronouncements. To put it differently, we can safely assume that the pro-active modernizers, personified in the Basque *emprendedor*, must have also produced a counterweight, expressed in the reluctance of the subaltern classes to be only subjects to the modernizing effort.

In the course of the last few decades a good number of international scholars and researchers, the majority of them social historians, sociologists and social anthropologists, have attempted to study and re-interpret the habits and self-conscious notions of subaltern classes as expressed in

---

the estate or the family home but also in rituals, such as sitting orders in the church, funeral rites and reserved cemetery plots in the church. In his study of traditional Gipuzkoan society Arpal also shows that one has to distinguish between different levels of nobility.

customs, norms and daily activities.[6] A similar paradigm change can also be observed in the Basque context. In what follows, I will briefly discuss some of the relevant studies and positions.

Marianne Heiberg's study *The Making of the Basque Nation* (1989) stands in the tradition of Basque community studies conducted by social anthropologists such as William A. Douglass (1975) or Sandra Ott (1981). Whereas Douglass looked at Murelaga (Bizkaia) and Echalar (Navarre), and Ott at Saint-Engrâce (Soule), Heiberg took a closer look at the community of Elgeta (Gipuzkoa). Like Douglass and Ott, Heiberg discusses ethnic forms of solidarity but she gives the topic a slightly different spin by pointing out that certain hierarchical forms and moral communities are not necessarily in opposition to each other. Furthermore, she maintains that the community's moral ideology cannot be explained solely by focusing on the issue of nationalism. In the postscript to her book (1989, 227ff) she tries to link moral ideologies to the equal exchange mechanisms that she sees clashing with rapid modernization processes. As in the case of Otazu's study of egalitarianism, Heiberg's new way of interpreting cultural patterns needs to be welcomed. However, I maintain that one can go even further than Heiberg by asking how these moral communities were actually institutionalized and embedded in daily actions and activities.

Within the new interpretative paradigm of studying common practices and belief, the social anthropologist Joseba Zulaika is arguably the most sophisticated of Basque scholars. Zulaika has emphasized the role that rituals, metaphors and 'secularized sacraments' play as symbolic constructions in everyday life (Zulaika 1988). He is interested in the subjective meaning and interpretations that individuals give to their actions. However, Zulaika would probably be the first one to agree with the argument that

6 This is not the place to go into all the details of the various approaches of studying the common people, their habits and their customs in past and present. Suffice to say, there is an ongoing international discussion of how to study history and society from 'below', and within the international debate a good number of national variations and positions, ranging from oral history to cultural studies, can be identified. For an overview see Peter Lambert and Phillipp Schofield (eds) (2004), *Making History: An introduction to the history and practices of a discipline*, Abingdon: Routledge.

many symbolic constructions are peculiar to the Basque Country and its social and cultural environment, but that it would be an exaggeration to suggest that all symbolic and meaningful constructions are used in what seems to be the main occupation and focus of analysts of Basque society and politics these days – that of nationalist discourse in its various political and violent manifestations.[7]

With his study of his hometown Itziar (Gipuzkoa), Zulaika has given us a study in which the actors and their subjective meaning come to life again. He has pointed us in the right direction when it comes to re-focusing the work on Basque society and culture and re-orienting it towards the study of collective meaning and luring it away from sensationalist or narrow-minded preoccupation with terrorism and nationalism. However, his own suggestions for a paradigm change – Zulaika is a keen advocate of *Basque Studies* – focus entirely on the so-called 'new anthropology' and 'cultural studies' and, important as these are, apart from a strong emphasis on the analysis of symbolic discourse not much is proposed in terms of a *conceptual* paradigm change. My point is that in order to re-focus research on Basque society and culture and in order to study the rich and already available empirical material, a different paradigm shift might seem necessary. I would argue that a dose of historical, economic, and institutional realism is necessary in order to explain and link again current meaningful rituals and communicative action with such apparently banal questions and daily activities like what it means to 'make a living', 'choose a home', or participate in 'leisure activities' (Robert S. Lynd).

As with social anthropologists, amongst social historians there is a movement away from doing traditional history that purports simply to study 'objective facts' and which follow the Rankean view of history 'as it really happened'. In the Basque context social historians, often focusing on daily life and local history, such as Felix Luengo (2001) and José Homobono

7 One should go a step further by questioning not only nationalist discourses but also the even more single-minded terrorism discourses, which have reduced an entire region and its population to the question of which side to take, either following the constitutionalist path or opting for political violence.

(1987, 1989, 1990 and 1997) have, through their work, given this new subjective, local and day-to-day dimension a proper foundation. Yet, apart from the occasional cross-reference or footnote to the larger conceptual framework – such as modernization in the case of Luengo or plebeian culture and moral economy in the case of Homobono – their attempts often seem to be locked into the local conditions and the local history they study. It is not suggested that their work gets lost in details; rather the important point is that their local social history writing rarely seems to report back to the larger issues of how to study social inequality and the subjective-collective challenges it poses to all scholars and researchers.

The point I would like to make is that engaging with the new insights from those local studies helps to paint a more comprehensive picture, particularly when it comes to the question of egalitarian myth and ethos and how they are linked to the issue of peculiarly Basque conditions and constellations, such as the common reluctance that can be encountered vis-à-vis modernization efforts. After all, it is only by virtue of comparative theoretical perspectives and universally applied concepts that singular events or unique constellations stand out.

Finally, we have to mention those social scientists and commentators who do not necessarily form a homogeneous group by any means (Aranzadi 2000, Juaristi 1987) but who share a common objective in that they have tried to study social change in the Basque Country by relating it to bigger intellectual ideas. In the view of these critical observers, living out a problematic collective memory or a century-old dream or fantasy is an ideological predisposition that often seems to go hand-in-hand not only with an unwillingness to modernize but also with a direct call to arms. However, while intellectual historians have looked at the Basque case, very often the sense for local peculiarities (for example, the Duranguesado in the case of Aranzadi) is only added on to the already existing larger picture (Christian millenarianism). Furthermore, how all this is then linked to present-day activities remains even more obscure. In other words, how it is possible that an historical imagination that is hundreds of years old is still being lived out at present is never really spelled out properly.

While all the approaches mentioned above have unearthed a wealth of historical, anthropological and sociological material, they have remained somewhat incomplete – and maybe necessarily so. My suggestion here is that a conceptual paradigm shift might produce other readings and may indeed lead to new insights by helping us to contextualize the rich empirical findings and interpret them differently. I will argue in this study that such a different observation point exists and that it allows us to interpret the available historical, social and anthropological material even better. More specifically and on the point of a paradigm change, I propose that the conceptual approach of E. P. Thompson and the insights of other social scientists such as Albert O. Hirschman are of primary relevance here. Applying Thompson's work on plebeian culture and moral economy allows us to follow and describe why and exactly how the egalitarianism ethos emerged. It shows, in other words, that it was not just handed down 'from above' and simply accepted. A Thompsonian perspective further allows us to see why such an ethos was maintained for such a long time and whether those historical-institutional expressions of plebeian culture and moral economy that were 'invented' a long time ago have survived and are still operational, or whether they are in crisis or are even in danger of becoming extinct. Such an historical evaluation and reinterpretation would allow us to study in more detail the subjective-collective dimensions that emerged out of unique class constellations. Furthermore, such a paradigm change would allow us to study class conflict and the conflict over resources in the context of local, regional and even national constellations, yet without denouncing them as mere attempts to find an answer to 'objective' historical expressions of ruling class behaviour or as mere historical 'consolidation processes' of new ascending classes striving for elevated and distinguished positions. In other words, a new approach would allow us to take a deeper look into what have been called Basque peculiarities or singularities yet without running into the danger of essentializing them and without reducing them or narrowing them down to a purely nationalist discourse.

Why in particular the work of E. P. Thompson? In his writings on late eighteenth-century England, Thompson has suggested that plebeian culture and moral economy were intrinsically linked. 'Plebeian culture' was an auxiliary term that he used to describe a situation where class was not what classic Marxist theory assumed it to be. Thompson proposed a paradigm shift away from the objective notions of class and class consciousness and towards studying subjective-collective dimensions such as the active contribution that the 'crowd' or the 'plebs' make to the common culture and customs. In his own writings and when studying older 'prototypes' or forerunners to the English working class, Thompson preferred to see these older classes in terms of fields of gravity, that is as heterogeneous constellations consisting of many dimensions and layers in which traditional popular customs played a major role. It was these customs in common that also helped to keep a moral economy alive – an economy which could take on various different meanings for the plebeian crowds such as common rights, norms or obligations, and day-to-day habits or practices, but which, taken together, in many ways constituted a force that was alien or opposed to the powers that be (Thompson 1980 and 1991).

Thompson was not the only scholar to write about plebeian culture and moral economy. The economist Albert O. Hirschman has provided us with an interpretation that I think fits perfectly well with Thompson's concerns. As Hirschman demonstrated in his work *The Passions and the Interests* (1977), early political economy was motivated by a strong moral impetus. Adam Smith, for example, was concerned with morality and in his study of political economy; he sought to advance moral behaviour – not to abolish it. Hirschman's interpretation of political economy was first fully expressed in *The Passions and the Interests*. Hirschman followed this up with a number of other studies in which he fine-tuned his general approach by inventing and using a number of closely related concepts such as 'exit', 'voice', 'loyalty', and 'commensality' (Hirschman 1970, 1982 and 1998). These concepts allow one to take a closer look at the micro-links that exist between political economy, customs and morals (Hess 1999). I would like to suggest here that, if applied to the Basque context and in the context of E. P. Thompson's larger notion of plebeian culture and moral economy, such an approach could provide maybe not so much another history 'from below' but at least a few new insights into the other side of the modernization process – something that so far has remained a conceptual black box for the historians, sociologists and anthropologists of the Basque Country.

I must immediately confess here that such an application also has its limitations, particularly when the historical material concerned does not provide enough evidence to write the 'thick description' (Geertz) of a given 'exit', a 'loyal' constellation or a clear 'voice' option. In the Basque case the available historical records are rich but unfortunately they do not provide sufficient detail to allow us to conduct a thorough economic study in the way Hirschman originally intended it. Despite this I will argue that a micro-level oriented and somewhat more 'liberal', less restricted conceptual version still provides enough guidance for the ordering and discussion of the available historical material and still lends itself to the discussion of the more macro-oriented ideas of the subaltern 'plebeian' culture and moral economy. I suggest here that it is indeed possible to combine the Thompsonian and Hirschmanian approaches – and even to add a critical institutional dimension to their perspective.

In what follows I will try to apply some of the crucial conceptual tools that Thompson and Hirschman have introduced to the history and sociological analysis of three particular institutions. There are of course many more institutions than the three selected ones, and others could have been chosen to illustrate Basque plebeian culture and to prove the point of the existence of a functioning moral economy.[8] In our case these three institutions have been selected because, as I will explain below, they have played a representative if not crucial role in Basque society and culture. When studied properly and in detail, they can be regarded as windows: once we look through them, they allow us to see the larger picture – namely some structural components of plebeian culture and moral economy in the Basque Country, a culture or an attitude that I decided to call 'reluctant modernization'.

The institutions that will be investigated are 1) the *baserria* (the Basque farmstead), 2) the *cofradía* (the fishermen's fraternity) and 3) the *txoko* or

8 The first institution obliterated that comes to mind is that of the Basque school, the *ikastola* and the various initiatives that helped to establish it. The author frankly confesses that to go into the peculiar history of education in the context of language is so complex and needs to be properly contextualized that it is beyond the possibilities of this study. For an account of this important movement, the discussions behind it, and its political implications, see the excellent studies of Jesús Arpal (1982) and Zalbide (1998).

sociedad gastronómica (the gastronomic or cooking society). Each of these institutions occupies a unique place in Basque natural environment, history, society and culture, including partly also the Basque diaspora. While the investigation of *baserri* culture allows one to study the countryside and the changes that occurred with industrialization, the *cofradía* allows the researcher to see the connection that the Basque Country has with the sea; finally, the *sociedades gastronómicas* are not as old as the other two institutions; they differ also in that they clearly represent a more recent and urban phenomenon and represent an effort to come to terms with urbanization and the more anonymous forms of modern life. In describing how these three institutions work, I suggest that they must be seen as expressions of a plebeian culture and institutional expressions of a related moral economy. Together they create a social habitus and a cultural disposition that is suspicious of modernization.

I will follow first and foremost a chronological order. The *baserria*, the institution that, as many historical anthropologists have stressed, points towards elements that existed before the middle ages, comes first. It is followed by the *cofradía*, which is in turn is followed by an analysis of the most recent institution, the *txoko*. The three main chapters follow the same overall logic. They are all 'thick descriptions', although not necessarily in the strictest Geertzean sense. First, a history of the institution and its environment is presented; this is followed by a functional account and an analysis of each institution's historical crisis, demise, failure or success. After discussing the history and function of each institution, I suggest that each also represents an ideal type or *modus operandi* of reluctant modernization. Thus, the *baserria* is interpreted as an institution in which the success of moral economy has always been limited by 'exit' conditions. In contrast, the *cofradía* has always had the facilitation of 'voice' as its main *raison d'être* – yet, as we will see, with only partial success. Finally comes the *txoko* or cooking society whose main function is to evoke a sense of 'loyalty' through creating 'commensality'. I have left it to my final remarks of each chapter and the more general interpretation at the end of this study to draw more general conclusions from the evidence presented.

I should stress here that this is a work of synthesis that relies on the empirical findings of other researchers. I do not dispute the factual evidence offered in the historical, anthropological, sociological or political literature that I draw upon. I very much cherish the fact that most of the studies that I have used and that I refer to were conducted in a solid social scientific way and provided me with sufficient empirical and historical material. What I would like to point out, though, is that while the studies concerned often provide plenty of evidence for my specific purpose, they do not give themselves a full answer to my leading concerns and questions. And why should they? It happens all the time that researchers follow their own unique epistemological interests, picking up different research questions or deciding consciously in favour of self-limiting visions that relate often to a concrete purpose or research interest. In the end I picked and chose those aspects which would help me to address my own epistemological concerns – plebeian culture and moral economy linked to the question of Basque peculiarities such as the reluctance to modernize. In other words, it is not new historical, sociological or anthropological evidence that I am looking for, but a new interpretation. While doing so I can only hope that in my attempt to look at something different I have not misrepresented the studies I draw upon, and I can only hope that this synthesis, in combination with the call for a more unifying, inter- and cross-disciplinary perspective, will be appreciated – particularly by those writers and scholars on whose work I have relied. Before delving into the historical material, I would like to finally stress that although this study relies in many ways on the work and insights of many other scholars and researchers preoccupied and concerned with the Basque Country, it is mainly based on my judgement and sociological imagination as they have been formed during more than twenty-five years of encounters with Basque culture and society.

I would like to point out that in most of my interpretation I limit myself to the portrait of the three institutions, *baserri*, *cofradía* and *txoko*, as they have emerged and developed in Hegoalde, the southern or Spanish part of the Basque Country. Occasionally, I will make references to Iparralde, the French part of the Basque Country, and to Navarre. The histories of the latter two are in many ways very different because they constitute a power in their own right (as in the case of Navarre) or pertain to another nation state and power (France in the case of Iparralde) with a completely different history.[9]

Throughout the text the spelling of names and places follows standardized Basque, *Euskera Batua*. There are deviations from *Batua* if and when the historical context or an authoritative source demands it, or where there is a known English use (for example, Navarre instead of the Spanish 'Navarra' or the Basque 'Nafarroa') or where there is a long-established French name or place in use (Bayonne, Labourd). In the case of Bilbao I have not rendered it to the Basque 'Bilbo', which is rarely used, even in areas where *Euskera* is the majority language. I have always adjusted the Basque noun depending on the use of the indefinite article (as, for example, in *baserri*), the definite article (*baserria*) or the plural (*baserriak*).

9 In many ways a case can be made that with the success of the French Revolution and the complete integration or domination (depending on the view one takes) of Iparralde, the distinct development of the French Basque provinces has probably reached a point of no return in terms of any possible unification of all the Basque territories.

CHAPTER 2

'Defending the Home': Moral Economy in the Rural Environment

It was at the beginning of the first millennium that denser and more concentrated rural settlements developed in the Atlantic zone of the Basque Country, usually located in close proximity to churches and cemeteries. The densest developments could be encountered in what today is part of the Basque province of Alava, a region that is close to the Cantabrian coastline but which itself has no coastal access. In terms of making a living in the rural countryside, milk production from pastoralism, particularly shepherding, dominated, usually supplemented by whatever the environment – mainly forest – could provide.[1] In terms of pastoralism one has to distinguish here between shepherds who engaged in transhumance and local sheep farming (Baroja 1971, 167ff). The former are referred to as *artzainak* or *pastores* with very special forms of cultural and social organization in terms of food supply, shelter and access to specific terrains and cross-border traffic, but also in terms of specific human survival skills, including the extreme circumstances of living in isolation for long periods. While the *artzain* (shepherd) is part of a larger shepherding community, he is for a considerable time also a lone guardian and often a lone traveller (apart from his dog). In contrast, the *labrador* (milk farmer) and also the

1 The first written historical document that has been preserved and that gives us at least a rough idea of what life was like in the early rural world of the Basque Country stems from the year 1025 and consists of a list of early rural settlements and zones (*aldeak*) in Alava. Probably written for the purpose of establishing or confirming tribute payments, it reveals the existence of shepherding and related milk production (Azkarrak et al. 2004, 218). It can be assumed that the development of rural *aldeak* precedes the time of the document probably by at least two centuries.

nekazari (peasant farmer) work mainly in close proximity to others and are territorially bound or limited to a specific terrain.[2]

Historically, pastoralism preceded farming;[3] it had its own unique social, cultural and even political representative forms and institutions. Communal rights and obligations and a sense of belonging helped to define unique *universidades* (rural units). The organization in form of *valles* (valleys) and *anteiglesias* (literally meeting places located in front of the church) corresponded to the needs and necessities of the shepherd community and also helped to link various communities together for such purposes as rights of transiting or roaming (Thalamas Labandibar 1935, 14ff). Once firmly established, such communities could also form economic units such as the *gaztandegia*, the collective that is dedicated to the production and marketing of cheese. Similar organizations were formed for the sale of *cordero* (lamb), *lana* (wool), *ovejas* (sheep) and, on a few occasions, also *vacas* (cows).

The first *nekazariak* still showed signs that they had emerged from a shepherding tradition; they were not accustomed to build or to reside in larger, permanent buildings.[4] They still lived in accommodation that resembled more provisional shelters, usually made out of readily available material such as wood, rocks and stones.[5] The peasant farmer and his family were always ready to move on and to work a different field if the soil did not

2 For a more detailed account of contemporary communal forms of Basque shepherding in Iparralde see Sandra Ott's study *The Circle of Mountains* (1993).

3 As Julio Caro Baroja has pointed out (1971, 152ff) the different Basque names for various mountain animals indicate that shepherding had indeed a long history that precedes modern times: *ardi* (sheep), *bildots* (lamb), *ahuntz* (goat), *segail* (small goat).

4 One should add here that the shepherd had his own *borda*, a form of sheltered accommodation, usually consisting of one large room. The whole construction resembled a hut rather than a proper house.

5 Baroja (1971, 113) maintains that the earliest construction material was most certainly wood because etymologically the word *baserri* derives from the word *basoa* (forest). *Baserritarrak* (those who live on farmsteads) first connoted most certainly people who were living in and made a living from collecting the fruits of the forest.

prove to be sufficient or showed some promise.[6] More stable conditions only emerged when convents, smaller churches and cemeteries were established and an adjunct network of smaller roads and paths developed – usually along the pilgrimage route to Santiago de Compostella.[7]

2.1 The *Baserria* – A 'Total Institution' in Historical Perspective

The development and establishment of simple housing constructions and shelters in the countryside first took place on the commons. Such settlements included the sharing of common meadows and mountain land between the occupants of the emerging rural villages and the surrounding *baserriak*. Later this land would become an integral part of the emerging property structures of the so-called seignorial powers and *hermandades* (Azkarrak et al. 2004, 224ff).

The twelfth century was crucial in this respect and marked a new epoch, with re-structuring and a new hierarchization of rural settlements. The valleys and their terrain became increasingly identified as distinct social, economical and political units. This process was accompanied by

6 It would be wrong to assume that the historical development from shepherding to organized milk production and later to agriculture meant that one activity replaced the other entirely. In the Basque Country we actually find a co-existence and often even a continuum between the three. To have more than one form actually improves alimentation and subsistence patterns. What can be said though is that the higher zones are naturally better for shepherding, while the lower zones are better for agriculture.

7 The pilgrims' way from Lourdes to Santiago can also be walked by taking alternative routes through the Basque provinces and Navarre. One can distinguish between a northern coastal route through Gipuzkoa and a part of Bizkaia and a southern inland route through Navarre. Both routes have also a few local variations before they reach Alava.

the founding and construction of urban towns and spaces.[8] By the late fourteenth century the Basque countryside had been transformed. No longer could one speak of an untouched or sparsely settled countryside. With seventy-one newly founded towns a dense network of communities had been established in which the countryside, town and village intersected in many ways, not least through shared access to the commons. Yet, even though the Basque countryside had been transformed considerably by these developments, it is important to recall that there were actually only two urban spaces that had more than 5,000 inhabitants, Bilbao and Vitoria; and, although the slow urbanization of the Basque provinces continued, the rural world continued to dominate the landscape for another six centuries. The most settled region in terms of both villages and towns in the countryside remained Alava, and, as we can see in the cases where documentation is available, the social structure of the average town still was very much linked to the rural environment. For example, in 1427, Laguardia (located in Alava) had the following social profile: clerics 4.46 percent, traders and artisans 3.23 percent, clerks, solicitors and lawyers 0.95 percent, *impotentes* 21.86 percent[9] and shepherds and peasants 69.77 percent (Azkarrak et al. 204, 295).

8 Three waves of the founding process can be distinguished: a first wave lasting until 1200, which was Navarrese in origin but which continued once Castile took over: Laguardia (1164), San Sebastián (1180), Vitoria (1181); a second wave established more towns between 1200–95: Fuentarrabía (1203), Getaria (1209), Motrico (1209), Zarautz (1237), Labastida (1242), Bermeo (1236), Plencia (1236), Tolosa (1256), Mondragon (1260) and Bergara (1265); finally, a third wave between 1295–1312, established the following towns: Durango (1297), Ermua (1297), Bilbao (1300), Portugalete (1322), Lekeitio (1325), Ondarroa (1327), Gernika (1366), Azpeitia (1310), Renteria (1320), Azkoitia (1324), Deva (1343), Eibar (1346), Elgoibar (1346), Zumaya (1347), Usurbil (1371), Orio (1379), Hernani (1380), Berorbevilla (1312), San Vicente de Aranzu (1308–19), Villareal de Alava (1333), Alegia (1337), Elburgo (1337) and Monreal de Zuya (1338) (Azkarrak et al. 2004, 280ff). Both the rural settlements and the increased urbanization process led to a further reduction in terms of forest space.

9 The origins of the word are difficult to track down. *Impotentes* could refer to either excluded minorities such as *agotes* or to other people who, for whatever reason, were not part of the strictly organized neighbourhoods (*vencidades*). For an historical

The establishment of towns and villages was paralleled by a consolidation process of the farmstead, the *baserria*, which was usually located outside but still within reasonable distance from the small rural town or village. Not only market exchanges bound the small town or village and the farmstead together but, probably more significantly, also communal property.[10] It is important in this context to notice the early signs of agrarian collectivism, usually expressed and organized in mainly church-inspired rural *cofradías* (brotherhoods). These brotherhoods helped to keep an eye on the field rota system and the harvesting and sale of produce stemming from the commons. It also dealt with the allocation of land, the prohibition of construction and the general protection of scarce resources (Thalamas Labandibar 1935, 40ff).

The history of the *baserria* as a more permanent building and its history as a more sophisticated social, cultural and economic institution begins only in the late middle ages, with agriculture becoming firmly established, and with lasting and purpose-built accommodation for which mainly oak wood and stone material were used (Santana and Otero 1993, 98). The first solid structures were fortified buildings that were particularly useful in fending off attackers. The early *casa torre*, erected between the eleventh and the fourteenth centuries, still resembled more a small fortress than a house used for farming purposes and rural exploitation. It was a relatively high-rise building with no windows or openings. It was freestanding and usually built close to similar buildings in order to form small settlements, providing some sense of security and mutual help in case of emergencies. By the first half of the sixteenth century a more peaceful environment allowed for the development of proper farmhouses, which no longer had

---

account of the role of *vencidades* and excluded minorities see Angulo Morales, A. and Reguera, I. (2004).

10 It is important to stress that, as an economic institution, the *baserria* was first and foremost an entity dedicated to communal survival and reproduction. It provided the manpower for the exploitation of the available common resources including those that the town or village shared with the surrounding farmsteads. More specifically, the farmstead as an institution provided for the extended family. Its main *raison d'être* was not to own property or to accumulate capital (Baroja 1986, 115).

to fear the constant threat from robberies and attacks. Several hundred such farmhouses were built around this period.[11]

At the early stages the *baserria* was almost exclusively located at the bottom of the valley; only later was it to move up the hill to become a spacious but frugal rural home. This farmhouse, referred to as the *casa solar*, was usually part of a smaller supportive infrastructure consisting of similar houses forming a small settlement, the *auzoa* (Lizarraga 1995). Later, with the arrival of corn (which eventually became a viable alternative to wheat), the *baserria* spread deeper into the forest, while farmhouses also developed nearer to the coast.

As to the construction type and architectural peculiarities, the early Basque farmhouses were very spacious, built with clearly designed separate functions in mind. While construction and materials varied according to landscape and immediate natural environment, most farmhouses had the same basic design: they contained a lower or ground floor which provided a space for family – with the kitchen and the fireplace as the centre of all human activities – and a stable for the livestock; the upper floor contained a common dormitory (later divided into two or more rooms to allow for more privacy); the attic was reserved for storing fruits and general harvesting purposes.

Over the centuries this type of farmhouse evolved slowly but steadily. The general rationale behind this long-term process was that form would always follow function. All serious work normally took place in the house or in the attached fields (Barandiaran 1925). With the increased division of labour and the differentiation of tasks came certain changes to the interior of the house. The cider press in the basement or on the ground floor became standard. The kitchen turned into an area where, apart from cooking and common eating, serious handicraft work took place, including basketwork, weaving, carving, carpentry and minor metal work. Inside the *baserria* these more sophisticated tasks needed more light, which led to major modifications and improvements particularly in the seventeenth and eighteenth

11 The very fact that a number of those houses still stand today demonstrates the high quality of the architecture and the materials used.

centuries. Higher and more vertical structures became the norm. More and bigger windows allowed for more natural light. Paved floors and balconies also became common features. In the 1930s electricity and running water arrived. However, despite the increased rationalization of the interior space of the *baserria*, the features of the Basque farmhouse remained basically unchanged: all the major tasks and indoor spaces remained under one giant roof.

In the Basque Country there exists a wide range of settlement patterns and, accordingly, access to the fields varies considerably. However, in general the surrounding fields are never far away from the *baserria* to allow for easy access. The size of the farmstead's land also varies, but with an average size of four to six hectares in the Atlantic zone it does not by any means resemble the *latifundio* structures that can be found in the south of Spain or the *minifundio* type for which Galicia is known. The typical *baserria* would be inhabited by a three-generational family, consisting of the (retired) grandparents, the *aita* (father, also the head of the *baserria*), the *ama* (the mother) and their dependants. Apart from the family that resides in the farmstead, the house would also provide shelter for the livestock, such as a small number of cows, pigs, chickens, and a number of other useful animals, usually a *txakur* (dog), an *idi* (ox) or a *zezen* (bull). Until the beginning of the twentieth century, animal husbandry would be limited and animals would mainly be used to either help with transport (oxen) or to provide milk and cheese for the *baserritarrak*.

The social life of the *baserria* would be dominated by fieldwork and family life. Depending on the location, the inhabitants would live a rather isolated and often solitary life in the case of the lone-standing *baserria*. However, usually a group of farmsteads would emerge to form a small settlement of neigbours (*auzo*). The *auzoa* would form a societal nucleus in which many things were done with the help of the neighbours, for example, maintenance work or the paving of access roads and paths or the common construction of churches or other small places of worship.[12]

12 In terms of daily life in the *baserria*, Julio Caro Baroja (1986, 256ff) has provided us with a portrait of the traditional *baserritarrak*. Between May and October the

It is difficult to pin down the different styles of the Basque farmhouses in terms of fixed or specific time periods. Many of the buildings relate or correspond to local and specific natural environments in which they were located. Following Santana and Otero (1993, 103 f), some basic forms and types can still be distinguished. The oldest type is the stone Renaissance farmhouse with four stone outer walls dating as far back as the sixteenth century. Buildings with an open trellis façade, constructed out of differently sized small wooden beams which supported each other vertically, became popular in the later sixteenth and seventeenth centuries. Around the same time wooden farmhouses developed where only the lower floor was made of stone; in some Basque regions some farmhouses were even built with integrated arched porches. In the early nineteenth century, the builders no longer saw a need for porches, mainly because the houses had now large windows and more light. Concerning the decoration materials that were used in the various periods, wood was mainly used in the sixteenth and seventeenth centuries and stone between the sixteenth and eighteenth centuries; iron was used too, but only for doors and the main *portal*.

Baroja distinguishes different architectural types by geographical distribution and natural environments rather than purely historical patterns (Baroja 1971, 111ff). For the Atlantic zone, which he defines as the fifty mile stretch that starts at the outskirts of Bilbao and ending in Biarritz and which today forms part of Bizkaia, Gipuzkoa, Lower Navarre and Labourd, stone and timber prevail as building materials. Located in an area with plenty of forest, the stone-beam construction is most commonly found here. To the south of this coastal zone and stretching as far as Navarre pure stone construction prevails. A mixture in terms of both architectural types and

---

baserritarrak would get up at 4.00 in the morning to prepare hay for the animals. This would be followed by a small breakfast at around 7.00. Between 7.30 and 12.00 they would work in the field. After lunch and a short *siesta* break, working the fields would continue until about 16.00. After another short break work would continue until 21.00, the time for dinner. The only interruption of the daily routine would be Sunday and *fiesta* days. For more details on the actual functioning of the traditional *baserria* in the twentieth century see Section 2.2.

natural materials used can be encountered in parts of Alava, Bizkaia and Soule.

Accordingly, the *meridional* type house consists mainly of stone and soil material with a relatively flat roof and can be encountered mainly in Navarre; the *medio* type is usually made out of stone, has a proper roof (tejada) and can be encountered in Bizkaia and Alava; the *pirenaico* type, which can be found in Soule is also made of stone but has a steeper roof. The *atlántico* type is the most common construction in Gipuzkoa, Labourd, Lower Navarre and Bizkaia and is made out of a stone, supported by wooden beams with a medium-sized roof on top.[13]

13 It is not hard to see behind Baroja's observation unique geographical and morphological patterns. Azkarrak et al. (2004, 383ff), for example, distinguish between three different general types and zones: firstly, the northern coastal area of what today forms the modern provinces of Bizkaia, Gipuzkoa and the northern part of Alava. This zone, roughly two-thirds of today's Basque Autonomous Community territory, is a zone where the *baserria* is surrounded by small fields and the forest has, until the arrival of modern times, provided the basic food supply for the rural population. Wheat production has been rare in this area. In this zone the soil has never been very rich; it has been the peasant farmer who makes it rich. In other words, what one can encounter in this zone is a certain artificiality through humanization: everything that one reaps and consumes is the result of hard human work and a very rational way of extracting the maximum out of limited and often scarce natural resources. In Basque there are numerous words that refer to the energy and hard labour that it takes to extract produce from the soil. Words that include the suffix – *aitz* (stone) are numerous, for example *aitzkor* (ax) and *aitzur* (hoe); another example would be *lan* (work) and the derivative *lain* (blossom). There are also numerous Basque names for a sophisticated variety of farm tools. Secondly, there exists a zone that covers central Alava and the western valleys. This zone is sometimes also referred to as the central or continental zone. The region's soil is good for growing cereals but also in its more mountainous parts shepherding has been common. In terms of territory, it covers approximately another third of today's Basque Autonomous Community. Thirdly, there is the southern Mediterranean zone including in its most southern part, the relatively wealthy Rioja region, with an extremely rich soil that owes its fertility to its proximity to the river Ebro. Here cereals and wine can grow in abundance (Azkarrak et al. 2004, 383ff). Azkarrak et al's description resembles an earlier one provided by Thalamas Labandibar (1935, 44f) who distinguishes between the region of the olive along the river Ebro in La Rioja, the region of cereals around Vitoria, the region of

The farmhouse itself – as we will see later, an economic, legal and religious entity in its own right – was given a name that usually expressed longevity or a clearly marked property, a long-term function or usage, a topographic location or a certain construction type. Usually every member of the family either residing in the *baserria* or associated with it were called or known by that name, for example names ending *-egi* refer to some form of livestock in a house, names ending with *-exte* indicate some human inhabitation and names ending *-enea* or *-ko* indicate some form of possession or property. Often a specific mode or profession can be expressed as well. Thus, *apezteguia* is the house where the priest lives, while *arosteguia* or *aretzena* is the house of the carpenter. Specific locations such as rivers, bridges, valleys, or a formation of trees can also be expressed in names (Baroja 1971, 111ff and 127ff).

Because of its independent, self-sufficient and autarchic character the rural *etxea* (house) or *casa solar* and its inhabitants invited the development of a whole ideology of equal and noble social standing usually referred to as *hidalguía universal* (Martínez Gorroriaran, 1993, 12ff). The Basque provinces, despite their internal differences and traditions (*Señorío* de Vizcaya – but *Provincias* de Alava y Guipúzcoa), were seen almost as a republic consisting of smaller rural republics that pertained formally to the King of Castile, but which had been granted special rights (*fueros*) by the throne which granted *de facto* autonomy of the Basque provinces in exchange for loyalty (Porres Marijuan, 2004, 237ff).[14]

pastures, corn and apple in Gipuzkoa, Bizkaia and parts of Alava, and the region of 'full agriculture' (wine, cereals, fruit trees) in Navarre.

14 This is not the place to go into all the historical details of the emerging provinces of the Basque Country and the related ideologies of egalitarianism and the defense of the home (*etxea*) as a unique space of or base for independence and freedom. Historically rich accounts and interpretative readings – although not always fully convincing, and sometimes also contradicting each other in parts – are provided, amongst others, by Otazu 1973, Aranzadi 1981, Martinez Gorriaran 1993, Porres Marijuan 2004 and Martínez 1994 (the last one being, by its own admission, more an interpretative reading than a proper historical account). From the accounts mentioned, I find Porres Marijuan's contribution the most reasonable and understandable historical account. Martínez's interpretation is interesting because he connects an

As briefly described above, the rural Basque farmstead developed over four long centuries, from the middle of the fifteenth to the middle of the nineteenth century (Lizarraga 1995, 184ff). During this time, *baserri* culture went through various phases and became subject to important changes. While the early developments were marked by strict hierarchies, the foundation of villages and towns, the introduction of orders and statutes for those villages and towns, the foundation of fraternities (*hermandades*) and *fueros*, and the increasingly dense network of the *baserriak* in general transformed life in the countryside. By the seventeenth century land in the Basque Country was fairly evenly distributed and families living on the farmstead were able to make a reliable living (Angulo Morales 2004, 181).[15]

Towards the beginning of the seventeenth century a crisis hit the coastal areas. The collapse of international trade affected Spain badly. The Basque

---

older discussion amongst historians with twentieth-century debates amongst social anthropologists. He also develops an interesting model of two types of formal and historical organization. According to his model, we can differentiate between an earlier stage of a *señorial* society, which is marked by lineage, blood relationships, parental relations and authority, including the passing on of noble names based on primogeniture inheritance patterns. Eventually this early model was replaced by the *foral* model. The *foral* model is based on the house as the important unit: in it, the actual residents are regarded as being more important than the family; additionally, the neighbourhood becomes increasingly important; finally, names are now related to the house, not the family, and the relationship with the past is not passed on through blood and family relations but through residing in the *etxea*. Martinez also makes clear that there is a continuum of debates about the role of the *baserria* and the sense of egalitarianism and freedom, starting from the early discussion by Garibay and Larramendi, leading to Rousseau and Humboldt, and finally to the modern political discourses such as Sabino Arana's, the *spiritus rector* of Basque nationalism, and academic contributions from social anthropologists, more often than not associated with *Estudios Vascos*.

15 It has to be added here that in the zones closer to the Atlantic the climate and the type of soil were not really good for growing cereals, which by then had become the main source of wealth. The farmers in these zones usually had to complement their income by producing cider, collecting chestnuts and forest fruits, or relying on additional small-scale cattle farming and meat or milk production.

provinces' trade and their overseas relationships suffered particularly. Not only was shipbuilding in deep crisis; more importantly, the blocking of ports had led to a crisis in wheat supply. The population of the Atlantic provinces, which from the fourteenth century onwards had discovered the advantages of living in close proximity to the sea – some form of involvement in either trade, shipbuilding or fishing was common – now reverted to the inland country, where more stable countryside conditions apparently prevailed (Angulo Morales 2004, 176). But the countryside and the limited amount of traditional crops it produced could only just provide sufficiently for the ever-growing population. A new crop from the New World, which had made its headway only slowly, provided the solution: corn.

It is fair to say that the introduction of corn radically influenced and changed the life and customs of the local rural population of the Basque provinces.[16] Compared to wheat, corn produced triple the volume of grain – thus contributing considerably to survival during the crisis (Santana and Otero 1993, 98f and Angulo Morales 2004, 176f). However, corn did not completely replace wheat. As late as the twentieth century the Atlantic provinces followed a crop-splitting regime with two harvests, one for corn and one for wheat. Despite the boom-and-bust cycles and the various crises that hit the countryside, the important point to make here is that for almost two centuries, roughly between the early seventeenth century and the end of the eighteenth century, the rural Basque world seemed to have enjoyed relatively stable and reliable structures. The Basque *baserritarrak* consisted overall, at least when compared to other European regions, of free and independent farmers and peasants. Only later, starting with the French Revolution and then increasingly during the course of the nineteenth century, would this situation be challenged and threatened, not only by political intervention and invasion, but also by industrialization and urbanization – in short, the arrival of the modern world (Enriquez

16 Until then the staple diet of the *baserria* in the Atlantic zone consisted of wheat, chestnuts, milk and milk products and, occasionally, white meat (sheep). The drink was mainly *sagardua* (cider). Potatoes, beans and corn only arrived with the discovery of the Americas, and even then it took another two centuries before these fruits were introduced to the Basque Country.

Fernandez, 1994). The process of modernization and the signs of change were more clearly visible in Bizkaia and Gipuzkoa. They developed into dual societies, urban and industrial on one side, rural and agrarian on the other. In contrast, throughout the nineteenth century and to large extent also during the twentieth century, Navarre and Alava remained, apart from their two big cities Pamplona and Vitoria, rural and agrarian (Urzainki Mikeleiz, 1994).

In many respects the problems that emerged in modern times were of a different sort and had to do with providing for the rural population and the small towns with somewhat limited means. The traditional two-family unit that formed the backbone of the *baserria* had a fairly high total output; yet, if calculated per person, the output appeared to be rather low. Furthermore, when used year in and year out, the soil inevitably became exhausted. Crop rotation provided only a partial solution. Also, expanding the range of produce helped. Thus, for example, in the Atlantic provinces cereals became less important while growing beans and potatoes was on the increase.

To avoid the further division of the already small and dispersed units of land that belonged to the *baserria* and which produced just enough to guarantee self-sufficiency, the ownership of the farmstead and land had usually been passed down as a whole. Subdivision between the inheritors would have eventually meant the death of the *baserria*. The traditional Basque inheritance pattern was that a single person was selected – in most cases the eldest son – to succeed the father as the head of the economic unit. Such a selection meant that the remaining siblings were at a disadvantage. These traditional inheritance patterns prevailed for centuries although they stood in stark contrast to the official Castilian inheritance laws, which were introduced in the early nineteenth century and which guaranteed equal rights to inheritance for all siblings.

Under the Basque custom of primogeniture, which continued to prevail even as modern times approached, it was traditionally the eldest son and his wife who became the new proprietors. It would be wrong, however, to assume that the Basque inheritance patterns and customs neglected the other members of the *baserria*. On the contrary, an egalitarian ideology prevailed to maintain the tradition of the indivisible farmstead, which worked to avoid the 'minifundization' of the land (the break-up into smaller and smaller units) and also to provide for the extended family. Thus, the new heads of the farmstead were still bound by a detailed inheritance contract which obliged the inheritors to provide for the parents who would continue to reside in the *baserria*, together with those remaining unmarried family members who decided to stay on and work in the farmstead (Urrutikoetxea 1992, 456ff). For those members who decided to leave, some form of compensation had to be found, either in the form of a single payment at their departure or a gift or a selection of gifts, such as pieces of the farmstead's furniture.[17]

Apart from such traditional inheritance patterns and customs, historians and rural sociologists have pointed out that in terms of general property relations, the *baserria* as an economic unit usually functioned well, with only minor differences related to whether the farmstead was owned or leased (Thalamas Labandibar 1935, Baroja 1986, Douglass 1970, Santana and Otero 1993).[18] This, however, is not to say that everyone was equal or that all *baserriak* functioned or operated along the same lines or rationale. Historical documents reveal some significant differences. The small upper class of *nagusiak* consisted of the most privileged individuals who usually owned several farmhouses; they did not work the land but profited from the produce that was generated on their estates.[19] The small and independent class of *etxejabeak* was dedicated to exploiting the resources of their own family homes and farmsteads. The biggest group was that of the *maizterrak*, the self-sufficient tenant farmers who did not

17 It should be stressed here that it was not always the case that the eldest son inherited the *baserria*. Since the logic was to guarantee the future functioning of the *baserria* as an economic unit and as a social institution, the inheritance could also go to an appointed person who was not the first son and direct descendant 'in line'. In cases where there was no eldest son, a sister could take over at the point of her marriage (to become the *etxekoandre*) or another family member was adopted to become the *etxekojauna*. For more details see Section 2.2.

18 'Functioning well' here refers to the time until the money economy was fully introduced and when the selling of land and farmsteads became an option to get rich.

19 In case of the *nagusiak* the traditional pattern of uniting or passing on properties was based on arranged marriages.

own but worked on farmsteads on the basis of renewable land contracts. Finally, there were the landless farm labourers and servants who worked on the farmstead in exchange for food and accommodation (Santana and Otero 1993, 99).

By the mid-nineteenth century, and despite signs of rapid modernization particularly in Bizkaia and Gipuzkoa, 80–85 percent of the Basque population still lived in rural areas. (Lizarraga 1995, 183ff). However, the shape of the rural Basque Country and the very notion of the countryside were very different now when compared to earlier centuries; the rural areas had become even more densely populated and new spaces continued to be claimed. Often rural towns and villages would offer land to its inhabitants and immediate *baserri* neighbours. There was also an increasing eagerness to settle in places that were located at a much higher altitude (600 metres and higher). The more mountainous regions and particularly the forest became increasingly subject to farm extension and exploitation. This also meant a further division and fragmentation of farm labour. Although labour on the Basque farmstead never involved being occupied with only one task, farming did become increasingly diversified. Hunting and collecting fruits of the forest, small-scale cattle farming, diversified milk production and *baserri* or *auzo*-based exploitation of coal, iron and wood were widespread.

While the farms made collective use of the resources available, they also marked the boundaries that were usually set by the other farmsteads. The farm soon reached the limits of its technical capacity and very often the future hung in the balance and depended on many factors such as political intervention, the sympathetic attitude of the political regime in power, rural exit to the developing urban areas and the Americas, the stage of local industrial development, and the further development of commerce or transport.

The coming of industrialization led to even more radical changes. The old moral economy, based on traditional customs, inheritance patterns and sustainability, was clearly in retreat. The landowning elite, by now an oligarchy of proprietors, lost its status and economic power, mainly because the peak in terms of maximum exploitation by absentee landownership in conjunction with traditional farming methods had been reached by the early nineteenth century. Despite owning various farmsteads and multiple properties, the farms were insufficiently rationalized and their stable output and growth rates were simply not strong enough to compete in an increasingly capitalist market. The reforms of the nineteenth century, which tried to turn communal land into private property, also had their limits. The two big groups or types of traditional farmsteads referred to above (those owning the land and those who were tenant farmers) had to cope with additional problems – the exit not only of its surplus family members who sought employment outside the *baserria* environment but also, increasingly, those *etxekoandriak* – the traditional heads of the *baserriak* – who began to offer their labour to the developing local iron, steel, paper and gunsmith factories; first as part-time workers and, as farming sank deeper into crisis, increasingly as full-time workers. By the 1930s the traditional workings of the *baserria*, its moral economy and culture that had defined Basque society for centuries, were no longer producing the necessary results in terms of social and economic sustainability.[20] While earlier collective forms of mutual help developed into full-flung cooperatives, which provided at least a part-time solution, the overall number of people working in the countryside and in *baserriak* was definitely shrinking (Thalamas Labandibar 1935, 60). Old tenancy regulations became extinct mainly because the available land did not produce enough. In the face of a major crisis those who were willing to remain *baserritarrak* tried to amend their circumstances by renting all accessible fields which they could possibly put to use productively and this was partly offered through the repartition of properties by its new owners or was available through negotiating with the local council. Be it through these measures, through the institutionalization of cooperatives or through the adoption of new farm machinery or new farming methods, none of it could stop the larger processes of the emerging crisis that were to

20 Such radical change of conditions also explains why hardly any new farmhouses were founded in the twentieth century. At the beginning of the twenty-first century old farmhouses have again become a sign of status and prestige and increasing overall modernization and wealth means that existing old farmhouses can now be freely purchased, renovated and preserved. Such a return to the countryside is a new cultural artifact; it is far from a revival of what was once a core institution of Basque society.

a large extent beyond the control of the *baserritarrak* – the depopulation of the countryside and the simultaneous industrialization and penetration of what was formerly a rural environment.

Already by the beginning of the nineteenth century the demand for radical change had found its political expression in liberal ideas. The liberals, who mainly stemmed from an urban environment and were particularly strong in Bilbao and its environs, argued against the traditionalist, usually rurally-based *carlistas*; the old form of life had become a hindrance and an obstacle to progress and it needed to be replaced by modern forms of trade and industry. Eventually the conflict resulted in the two Carlist Wars, which in the end led to the abolition of the old laws, traditional customs, old borders and related tax regimes. *Baserri* culture was to survive for another half a century but by the beginning of the twentieth century the overall picture had changed almost beyond recognition. The long medieval age that had lasted in some parts of the Basque Country until the end of the nineteenth century finally disappeared.

Despite the obvious crisis and the visible decline that hit the *baserriak* even before the beginning of the twentieth century, the ideology persisted that countryside, *baserri* and Basque culture were entwined, almost to the extent that they could be perceived as being identical (Lizarraga 1995, 180f). As a matter of fact, exactly at the time the old rural world came seriously under threat from industrialization and urbanization, in short, from modernization – in the Basque Country usually identified with urban Bilbao and its environs – the founder of the Basque nationalist movement, Sabino Arana y Goiri, argued that the rural culture should not be forgotten but needed to be rediscovered. Following Arana y Goiri, the *baserria* as an institution came to be seen as the heart of the authentic Basque homeland, an institution associated with noble status and freedom. Its pillars were seen as the house or homestead, the extended family, paternal authority and religion (Lizarraga 1995, 181).

Like any idealized view, the romantic call for a return to the values of the half-forgotten rural world refers to both real and imaginary experiences. While it was certainly true that the *baserria* and the extended family had become the basic unit, not only in an economic sense but also in the sense of social and political reproduction and economic gain, acknowledging the institution that the *baserria* had become also meant the wilful acceptance of the inherent contradictions that came with it, such as the acceptance of an old-fashioned moral economy, subsistence patterns without any hope of growth, an unequal inheritance pattern and the inevitable emigration of surplus family members. The inherent contradictions were not only accepted by the Basque political elite that, inspired by Sabino Arana, would eventually form the Basque Nationalist Party, but also by the intellectual movement that was the *Estudios Vascos*. The two congresses that the organization celebrated in 1918 and 1920 explicitly addressed rural problems and in particular the situation of the traditional *baserria*, promoted by the intellectuals as the main reproduction cell of Basque culture. Suggestions for reform were limited to an increased diversification of produce and products (milk and meat mainly) and the internal rationalization of the farmstead (sanitary conditions, solid construction of farm buildings, proper floors and so on). No suggestions were made in terms of real structural *baserri* and environmental changes (Urzainki Mikelaiz, 1994). The main reason seemed to be that nobody wanted to dismantle the core institution of Basque society. It was as though criticizing the traditional *baserria* and arguing for major agricultural reform would be seen as aiming at the destruction of Basque culture. Eminent social anthropologists such as Barandiaran and Aranzadi, together with the *Estudios Vascos*, had again and again stated that the Basque farmstead represented what Lévi-Strauss has called the 'structural components of *la maison*' and Marcel Mauss a 'total institution' in the sense that the *baserria* combined livelihood, culture and economics; yet the same Basque social anthropologists also insisted that these patterns had existed since time immemorial. This historical primordialism was also applied to important moral components such as the aspects of equality and freedom (Martínez, J, 1994). As it appears, the will to reform was limited by the struggle for cultural survival.

It would probably be wrong to explain the continued existence of the Basque farmstead only by referring to ideology. Seen from a purely functional perspective, for most of the long nineteenth century and the first two decades of the twentieth century, the typical formation of *baserri*-plus-aggregate-family structure allowed for maintaining old customs and for moderate reform (Urrutikoetxea 1992, 452ff). Family arrangements such a primogeniture patterns served as a regulator, as a 'demographic break' against overcrowding or uncontrolled expansion of those who lived on the farmstead. The arrangements were often complicated and costs could be high. They included long search periods for an adequate partner who would be prepared for life on the *baserria*; this in turn often led to relatively late marriages. A considerable number of solitary women who could not, for whatever reason, become part of the inheritance deal were compelled to leave the *baserria*, to move into town or become part of the institutionalized church as nuns. The number of solitary men was even higher. In contrast to the solitary women they had more options in that they could become either helping hands in the *baserria*, join the military or opt for emigration (usually to America). Yet, there was also reluctance to follow such a model slavishly. Giving birth before marriage was one often-sought form of creating facts; others included internal 'economical' solutions such as splitting or increasing rotation of the fields for an increased market-oriented output that would provide for all members. New forms of credit systems sprang up that can be described as 'clan'-like relationships whereby a relation working in the town provided credit for the needy brother. Whatever the solution consisted of, men had a clear advantage. At the beginning of the twentieth century it was still easier for a man to get a job in the town or city, to live a bachelor's life or to have illegitimate children. Yet all these 'private' solutions could not in the end provide endlessly for what constituted a major crisis, the saturation of the countryside. There came a point where it became impossible to have more *baserriak* and more functional marriage arrangements while at the same time the surplus population moved to the next village, town or city.

2.2 Function and Crisis of the Traditional *Baserria*

No description of the essential functions of the traditional *baserria* and their impotence in terms of providing an appropriate answer to the modernization crisis can be complete without reference to the two studies that the American anthropologist William Douglass conducted in the mid-1960s (Douglass 1970/2003 and 1975).[21]

On first impression, the traditional farmsteads of the two Basque towns studied, that of Echalar (Navarre) and Murelága (Bizkaia), seem to be very similar.[22] In both cases empirical evidence suggests a model of

21 The studies appeared in reverse order in relation to the fieldwork conducted. The comparative investigation of two Basque communities, Echalar (Navarre) and Murelága (Bizkaia) was part of Douglass's doctoral research and was carried out between 1963 and 1966; however, it was only published in 1975. The study of funeral rites and how they represent the functioning of the *baserriak* in Murelága emerged in the context of the doctoral research but took on a momentum of its own. It was published in 1970, five years before the doctoral dissertation appeared in print.

I agree with José Ramón Mauleón (1994a and 1994b) in that the classic studies of Douglass (1970/2003 and 1975) and Etxezarreta (1977) must be seen as belonging to the most important contributions to the study of the traditional *baserria*. However, I think that Mauleón goes too far in his emphasis on economic causes, particularly when he sets Douglass's anthropological work (and Greenwood's exogamic cultural explanation) against Etxezarreta's economic approach. My reading of Douglass is that he talks on numerous occasions about how the traditional *baserria* has become dysfunctional in the modern capitalist system. One could even argue whether Etxezarreta's study does not focus too much on economic rationality and not enough on other explanations such as the ones provided by Douglass. I will refer to Etxezaretta's work later; at this point I would just like to stress that I see much more continuity between the two studies than Mauleón suggested.

22 For my purposes I am reading both studies that Douglass conducted as one. I take the comparative study of Echalar and Murelága to be the more comprehensive work while I find the study of funeral rituals in Murelága more restrained in the sense that it tries to demonstrate how one important function, that of maintaining the *baserria*, contributes to the reproduction of the entire structure. Therefore, in my account, this second study of funeral rites serves mainly as an 'information adjunct' to the first comparative and more comprehensive study. I am aware of the fact that this

concentric circles surrounding a core. In Echalar this core is a single dwelling, the actual *baserria*; in Murelága it is actually a nucleus of farmsteads – the *auzoa*. The circle immediately surrounding the core consists of cereal lands, which require the most intensive labour and dedication; this circle is surrounded by a second circle which needs less attention, the meadows that provide the hay for most of the small number of farm animals; the last circle consists of mountain land, usually forest and space for pasturage (Douglass 1975, 18ff). In terms of average size, both *baserria* types comprise between 5 and 15 hectares. Exceptions in terms of larger land holdings exist but this is mainly an excess of very steep and mountainous land that for the most part cannot be used productively for farming purposes. Both *baserri* types have some lifestock that guarantees some cash income from milk or milk-related products. Apart from a few cows (there are usually less than half a dozen), each *baserri* has some pigs, chicken, sheep, occasionally goats and usually a larger animal that is used for utility purposes such as transport, be it either a mule, an ox or a horse.

As to the structure of the nucleus of the model, the *baserria* and its inhabitants,[23] the domestic group occupying the farmstead usually consists of the three-generational family, the *etxekoak*, which includes a senior married couple, a junior married couple and their (unmarried) children.[24] It

---

does not do the book full justice in terms of its main subject – funeral rites. For my purposes, its information benefit is that it highlights some aspects not mentioned in greater detail in the comparative study, such as the *aldea*, the entire community district of Murelága.

23 In the previous chapter we already addressed the question of the internal architecture of the *baserria* and its improvements over the centuries, so there is no need at this point to refer to it again. As we will see later, a further rationalization took place in the course of the twentieth century; however, as distinct from the improvements in the past this new form would not come from within but from without.

24 At the time Douglass conducted his research, he found that the three-generational family was no longer the paradigmatic model to follow; only about a fourth of the domestic groups had three-generational families living in the *baserria*. In fact, the statistics showed that in reality the two-generational family had become the most prominent type (encountered in around two-thirds of all households in Echalar and Murelága) (Douglass 1975, 37 and Douglass 1970/2003, 131).

is not unusual for the unmarried siblings of the heir to stay at the *baserria* and submit themselves to the authority of the family head. Those siblings who marry leave the house but are usually compensated in one way or another for relinquishing all their rights concerning the farmstead (Douglass 1975, 33ff and Douglass 1970/2003, 135ff). The complex marriage and inheritance arrangements have for a long time been given legal status in Navarre and in Bizkaia through so-called *fueros*, special rights that take precedence over the Spanish Civil Code, which, in reform-oriented and modernist Napoleonic fashion, calls for equal division amongst the heirs. These *fueros* must be regarded as a conscious way or act of preserving the traditional and mainly rural way of life.[25]

The handing over of authority in the *baserria* happens at the time when the heir, usually the eldest son who has been socialized into taking on this role, has found a wife and the couple get married (Douglass 1970/2003, 137ff).[26] The inheritance contract that is being put together on this occasion spells out in detailed fashion all the rights and obligations that the new *etxejaunak* have, especially vis-à-vis the retired parents who continue to reside at the farmstead, but also concerning those who do not inherit the *baserria* and who must be taken care of or compensated.[27]

25 The traditional inheritance system guarded by the *fueros* would collapse at a later stage because of its inability to respond adequately to changing conditions and modernization. Had Spanish laws been fully applicable in the Basque Country, the traditional *baserria* and its world probably would have collapsed a long time ago.

26 It is only when the parents die that the inheritance arrangements earlier agreed come fully into force. It is the final rites of passage and 'passing on' that are the subject of Douglass's study *Death in Murelága*.

27 The system relies very much on the existence of an extended kin network. In terms of inheritance, clear preference is given to the criteria of descent, residence on the farmstead and the existence of a marriage tie (Douglass 1975, 34 and Douglass 1970/2003, 118ff). Sometimes these arrangements do not work the way they were planned, be it because of the absence of a male heir, an individual decision of the designated heir or just simple natural circumstances. Douglass (1970/2003, 135) has drawn up a list of such often occurring possibilities: no son is available, the eldest son remains a bachelor, the eldest son emigrates, the first child is a daughter, or the oldest son dies prematurely. In such circumstances quasi-members can be co-opted into the *baserria*.

The new heirs form the core of the *baserria*; the male head is known as *etxekojaun* (literally, 'lord' or 'master' of the household), while the woman at his side is called *extekoandre* (literally, 'lady' of the household). Between the two there is a clear division in terms of responsibilities. The *etxekojauna* makes all the important decisions related to managing the farmstead. Because of the demands of this role, the person in question should be 'sober, hard-working, and little given to recreation' (Douglass 1975, 40).[28] The *extekoandre* should complement the husband and support him in his role. In terms of labour, some division but also some overlapping exists. The *etxekojauna* usually carries out most of the more physically demanding farm work but it is very common for his wife to help considerably in carrying out this work, including even the most physically demanding tasks.

As Douglass has pointed out in his study on funeral rites, it is more important to keep the *baserria* alive as an institution than to reproduce and prolong immediate blood and family ties (Douglass 1970/2003, 122f).

Bearing the evidence of change from a three-generational to a two-generational family in mind, Douglass explains that 'the vagaries of life demand certain flexibility. Over time, the domestic group membership is subject to contraction and expansion as the persons are born, mature and depart, and die. At any particular moment a domestic group may be unable to utilize all of its *baserri* resources properly or, conversely, may have been expanded beyond the carrying capacity of its farmstead' (Douglass 1975, 39). Douglass concludes his remark with a powerful (and soon to be realized) prediction: 'Today's expanded domestic group may well prove to be tomorrow's cripple' (ibid.). Douglass also notes that, all things being equal, the normal procedure in Mureléga is to prefer male primogeniture, the oldest son inherits, whereas in Echalar there seems to be no clear preference in terms of the profile of the heir, neither age or sex is decisive (Douglass 1975, 43). In the case this arrangement does not work, one can always refer to co-optation through adoption or appointment. The co-opted members are known as *familije*, referring to those who are not necessarily bound by marriage but who become part of the *etxekoak*, those who help to maintain and reproduce the *baserria* as an institution. As Douglass points out, even a place in the floor (*sepultura*) of the local church might be reserved to those co-opted members of the household (Douglass 1970/2003, 118f and 155ff).

28 Douglass also points out that in Basque culture very little esteem is given to people who do not fit this picture, particularly those who are inclined to opt for an easy life style.

In some cases it is common for the wife to deal with all necessary money transactions and give the man pocket money (Douglass 1970/2003, 141). Children are usually socialized from an early age to follow in the footsteps of their parents – particularly the eldest son where stronger primogeniture traditions prevail as in the case of Murelága. Until they reach the age of thirteen or fourteen and leave school, few demands are made of them. As to the unmarried siblings who reside in the *baserria*, they fully take part in the daily work. Depending on their sex, they either support the *etxekojaun* or the *etxekoandre*. The relationship between brothers is most important and, while growing up, is usually marked by friendship. However, at a later stage because of the inheritance situation and potential conflicts over pay-outs the relationship can become strained (ibid., 119ff and 150ff).

The role that the *baserria* plays as an institution goes beyond mere economics. There is a total identification of house, terrain and home (Douglass 1970/2003, 31). Usually the *baserria* remains linked to one particular family of occupants for generations and almost becomes a timeless institution. Individuals related to one particular farmstead, independent of whether they reside in it or not, are known to others by the name of that *baserria*.[29] The only minor difference relates to whether the *baserria* is leased or owned. In Murelága most of the farmsteads are owner-occupied; in this constellation the case seems to be straightforward since farmstead and family are identical. In contrast, in Echalar where renting is much more common, the name of the *baserria* moves with the family in case economic pragmatism demands transferring to another rented property (ibid., 48).[30] The difference between renting and owning a *baserri* is minimal; the only difference usually pertains to the rights of the forest fruits and the costs

29 As Douglass stresses, in this respect the Basque farmstead differs from the farmstead in Ireland where the farmstead takes the name of the family (Douglass 1970/2003, 31).

30 As a matter of fact, in the case of strong primogeniture tradition, as in the case of Murelága, one could analyse – just as Douglass has done – the functioning of an entire town just by studying Basque funeral rituals as rites of passing on *baserri* relations (Douglass 1970/2003).

of maintaining the *etxea*, the main house, both of which the actual owner takes care of.

After the description of the inner core we turn now to the concentric circles that surround the core and the different relationships that exist between the core and its environment. Douglass's diagram formalizing Bizkaian and Navarrese *baserri* practices shows that the two are almost identical – with one important variation: in the Murelága model the core consists of a small community, a nucleus of farmsteads called the *auzoa*, while in Echalar the settlements of the *baserriak* are more dispersed and usually form relatively isolated entities (ibid., 18ff). What is not immediately visible from the more abstract model is that there exist in reality important variations in the relationship between core and environment. To put it differently, there are very different settlement patterns and different ways of accessing the commons in the two rural communities. In reality, the type of core partly determines the different relationships to the surrounding circles. As we will see, it is these different patterns that partly help to explain some of the different features and dynamics of the two communities (Douglass 1975, 52ff).

While agreeing in principle that the model consists of a core and of concentric circles surrounding the core, a distinction needs now to be drawn that helps to understand the different social and economic consequences of geographic land distribution. In the case of Murelága, and because of the unique formation of the *auzoak*, some of the fields that on first impression seem to be very close to the farmstead are actually not located in the immediate surrounding but are much more dispersed and therefore harder to reach. The irony is that it is exactly this dispersed form which allows for more neighbourhood co-operation and face-to-face interaction (Douglass 1975, 60ff; Douglass 1970/2003, 36ff). The interaction between the *baserriak*, which forms part of the *auzoa* culture, can take on the form of *auzorik hurrena* (assistance to and from the immediate neighbour in case the *baserria* is somehow in crisis or threatened, as in the cases of flooding, emergency repairs, rescuing animals, etc.) or the *auzo*-wide practice of the *bisita* (a visit in the case of good news such as birth or marriages or tragic personal circumstances such as accident or death). Somewhere in between lies a third form of mutual help and consultation which any of the smaller subgroups, for example three or four *baserriak* in a specific location, might find to their mutual advantage.[31] Beyond such informal ways, common *auzo* activities involve not only common infrastructure projects such as buildings and maintaining small access roads and paths but also include cultural and religious activities, such as maintaining the local chapel, running a small tavern for recreational purposes or organizing the local *fiestas*. If the hamlet is big enough a *mayordomo* (caretaker) may be selected to represent the local *etxekojaunak*. His task – in this role he is usually supported by the *etxekoandre* – is to take care of the local chapel building, certain chapel services (most important in the case of funeral arrangements), or to function as a treasurer or bookkeeper, and occasionally as the contact person or speaker for the neighbourhood. In modern times the *auzoa* has also become an agency for change, demanding or suggesting improvements such as plumbing and electrification.

In contrast, in Echalar the same amount of interaction is not required simply because the layout of the fields is usually closer to the ideal type: land that is contiguous to the individual *baserriak* and does not include outfields some distance away from the core *baserriak*.[32] Despite geographical

31 In her study of a Basque shepherding community in Sainte-Engrâce in Iparralde, Sandra Ott has encountered similar forms of mutual help. For a more detailed account see Ott (1993, 63–81, 117–130, and 213ff).

32 Referring to the work of Julio Caro Baroja, Douglass explains the difference in type with ancient roots of settlements (Douglass 1975, 55). Linguistic evidence from *baserri* names suggests that the *korta* type is the older form and goes back to a period when agriculture was first introduced. The *korta* settlements were individual and isolated dwellings before land became densely settled. In contrast, the *borda* type refers back to pastoralism and means a shelter that pastors used. It is probably not as old as the *korta* type settlement, which dates back to the sixteenth century.

In terms of differences, historical sources and linguistic evidence also seem to suggest that the *baserriak* in Echalar are actually younger in terms of historical development than the type that one can encounter in Murelága. Douglass points out that 'the history of rural settlements in Echalar ... presents a pattern of gradual extension into more remote reaches of the village terminus as new farm units were carved out of former wilderness and pasturage areas. This may be contrasted to the apparently simultaneous and ancient founding of the rural *auzoak* in Murelága' (59). He suggests in the end that 'the rural settlement in the two villages developed along dissimilar

and historical differences mutual assistance is offered in Echalar, too; it is just organized in a slightly different way because of the unique geographical and historical patterns of the Navarrese environment (Douglass 1975, 65ff). As in Murelága, the Echalar community knows the *bisita*, the visit to bring good personal news or in reaction to tragic circumstances. Because individual farmsteads are more dispersed and do not, in most cases, form a nucleus, social contacts do not develop naturally with the *auzo* neighbour but according to the needs of the individual *baserria*. The farmstead communicates most easily with the geographically closest *baserria* in the country. However, the interaction of the more dispersed individual farmsteads with the closest farmstead resembles that of the *auzorik hurrena* in Murelága. In Echalar it is called *lehenbiziko atea*, 'the first door' that can be encountered next to the property (66f). The help and assistance provided cover the same range as in Murelága. Another expression of the mutual benefit system is the *txerri puskak*, referring to 'the parts of the pig'; that is, once an animal is slaughtered – it does not have to be a pig – parts of the animal go to the surrounding farmsteads. This form of sharing is part of a system of gift exchanges; the favour is usually returned eventually. It should be mentioned though that the form of exchange is not as frequent as any of the other types of interaction mentioned, mainly because of the distances between the more dispersed and isolated farmsteads in Echalar.[33]

In terms of relationships between the core and its environs the two communities studied also differ in the way they regulate access to and use of the commons (71ff). Usually each village has some commonly guarded land that can serve a variety of purposes. In the case of Echalar the commons provide access to the forest, which in turn guarantees access to wood, which in turn can be used as charcoal – a common practice in the Navarrese community. Commonland may also be used for pasturing sheep, cows or horses, or harvesting the fern that grows on the common land to be used as

---

lines, but by the middle of the last century the systems as we know them today were in existence. Similarly, by the middle of the last century the *baserria* pattern of settlement in the two villages reached its zenith prior to entering into a period of twentieth century decline' (ibid.).

33 Again, similar forms of mutual help are described in Ott (1993).

fertilizers. There are also some tax benefits or returns related to the use of the commons, particularly in the case of granting grazing rights or having mutual agreements with neighbouring shepherd communities. In contrast, the commons in Murelága, which are considerably smaller and also include some land that cannot be used (rock cliffs), do not provide such means. Murelága's main communal source is actually some forest reserves, consisting mainly of pine trees, and also a marble deposit that was discovered in the 1960s and that has been quarried for the community.[34]

We have looked with an almost Weberian eye – in the sense of a snapshot-like ideal type – at the *baserria* and its environs and the relationship between the two. It is now necessary to take account of how the traditional *baserria* managed to cope with accelerated change and how it tried to survive in the dynamic environment of the twentieth century. In order to do so, Douglass distinguishes between three periods (Douglass 1975, 86ff).

34 In order to fully appreciate the present situation (1960s) of the commons Douglass is talking about, it is necessary to know that a law that was introduced in the nineteenth century (*Ley de Desamortización*, 1855) demanded that the local municipalities give up the large holdings that were in their possession. This meant that some of the better land was given away to local *baserriak*, therefore diminishing the commons to some of the worst land available – apart from forest land (Douglass 1975, 80). The situation was not helped by the fact that the Basques were on the losing side in the two Carlist Wars. The commons were mainly used to pay tribute to the victors. It should not come as a complete surprise that this led to the near bankruptcy of many local councils and municipalities, amongst them Echalar and Murelága. Both events, the new law and the Carlist Wars, led to long-term complicated conflicts over scarce resources. In the end the solution in terms of putting the commons to beneficial use was better in Echalar where individual *baserriak* completely absorbed parts of the commons and treated it as private property, creating clear-cut responsibilities as to the common land and thus avoiding conflict. In contrast, in Murelága there was considerable disagreement over complete free access to the remaining commons *(-usaak)* and a system that puts the use of the commons under the control of individual *baserriak*, called *baso mojonauek*, creating a difficult situation in terms of property and access rights and leaving the commons as the poorest land in the village (80f). However, it is important to stress in this context that the commons in Echalar, due to the size and quality of land, always played a much larger role than in Murelága (Douglass 1975, 83).

The first period lasted from the beginning of the twentieth century to 1925. This period can be regarded as an extension of the long Basque nineteenth century in the sense that work patterns in the *baserria* continued to remain labour-intensive. The *baserritarrak* continued to rely on farm tools that in other places had already disappeared. The plough and the scythe remained unknown or were little used. In order to work the fields, the *baserritarra* had to rely on his own labour power, and, periodically, on the labour power of his *auzo* neighbours. The crops planted and grown continued to be mainly cereals, beans and chickpeas. In terms of garden vegetables, green beans, cabbage, onion, garlic and leeks were the staple produce and diet. The potato was known but still had not assumed the role it would play at a later stage. Animal husbandry seems to have been limited to subsistence levels for which the Pyrennean cow had become a symbol: not demanding much attention, it could be left to its own devices; it could be used for occasional labour tasks and it produced just enough milk for the *baserritarrak*. In the more mountainous parts one could encounter sheep and sometimes also horses. The diet of the *baserritarrak* was usually supplemented with apples and chestnuts. Apple orchards could also be used to produce cider. Concerning the forest reserves, Douglass notes one major change that had important repercussions (Douglass 1975, 88f). At one point the local forest, particularly the oak and chestnut trees, had become infected with a particularly virulent disease. As a remedy and partial replacement pine trees were planted. The unexpected outcome was that the pine trees grew extremely well in the local climate (the trees were first planted mainly in Bizkaia) and turned into a major source of income for the Murelágan *baserriak*. However, growing pine trees also led to a major argument between the new pine growers and traditional sheep farmers, since the sheep tended to enter the new pine plantations and destroy them.[35] It was almost impossible to fence off all trees but it was also impossible to guard the sheep all the time. In the end, the local council decided to side

35 Douglass points out that in the 1970s the conflict had still not been resolved. Douglass does not discuss another scenario – that of relatively dense and dark pine forests leaving little space and light so that sufficient grass for grazing sheep can grow.

with the more profitable pine growers, to the detriment of sheep farming, which became almost extinct.

Overall, it could be said that the first period was marked by the absence of a dominant money economy. Money was important as a source of wealth, something 'to be hoarded, not enjoyed'; it was still regarded as 'an end in itself' (Douglass 1975, 93). Modern capitalist logic and pecuniary culture had not penetrated every aspect of rural life. The *baserria* continued to function very much along traditional subsistence levels, although some changes – as in the case of the growing pine trees as capital or inheritance reserve – were notable. In terms of household provisions, very few ingredients or items stemmed from outside the farmstead; this applies to coffee – still very much seen as a luxury item and to be consumed only a few times per year – as well as sugar, spices and alcoholic beverages other than cider, all of which had to be bought. Items such as clothing and most of the furniture continued to be produced on the farmstead. Modern infrastructural improvements such as running water and electricity became available later and therefore made no major financial demands. Reflecting on this early twentieth century period, Douglass concludes that

> subsistence farming and household self-sufficiency were both a 'moral' way of life and a means of preserving one's independence from the incursions of the outside world, and particularly the market-place. The *baserritarra* entered into commerce once the basic needs of the domestic group were met, but not before. Even then he generally entered the market as a seller, not as a buyer (Douglass 1975, 93).

Two major things changed during the second period (1925–45) and both impacted on household patterns in the Basque farmstead considerably (Douglass 1975, 93). The first major change seems to the modern reader only a minor technological revolution; for the *baserritarrak* it meant introducing radically new cropping and farming techniques. The use of the scythe, which replaced the sickle, and the introduction of the modern plough, constituted massive and immediate improvements in terms of labour efficiency.[36] The second major change came through the consumption of prefabricated consumer goods such as livestock feeds and fertilizers, which made life easier but also more expensive in terms of cash requirements. It also meant entrance into commerce, since these provisions were only available through purchase. This in turn meant that the *baserria* had to produce more for the market and go beyond subsistence levels in order to generate money. In the two cases studied, Echalar and Murelága, this meant a more intensive output by resorting to increased milk production. It has been pointed out above that the Pyrenees cow had already become a symbol for subsistence farming; the purchase of Swiss cows, which produce more milk than the Pyrenees type, initiated a change in attitude and production (94). The now widespread use of the scythe helped; it was less time-consuming to cut the necessary hay for the stabled animals. Notable was also an increased substitution of cereal and mountain land for meadows and an even more intense use of the meadowlands through the use of fertilizers. As an immediate result, wheat production declined considerably. Another change related to the different use of the commons which, as pointed out earlier, were still significant in Echalar, where pastoralism, especially sheep farming, continued to play a major role but which were now almost insignificant in Murelága where an actual abandonment of the commons has been seen (96). What also differentiated Murelága was the total substitution of pine growing for sheep farming, with lumbering becoming the major source of private *baserri* income.

The rationalization of work in the *baserriak* in both villages, by means of increased efficiency through the use of the scythe, all-year round stabling of farm animals, and milk production, was accompanied by other important developments, in particular the changing role of women in the household (96f). Women no longer produced all the clothes and did not do all the preparatory work in the kitchen such as turning raw produce into edible provisions. Thanks to the introduction of electricity and other inventions which transformed kitchen work, time spent in the kitchen was steadily

36 This relatively late introduction might be due to the steepness of much of the terrain.

reduced. The diet also changed considerably and consumables which had previously been regarded as luxuries – ready-to-consume olive oil, coffee, sugar, chocolate, and alcoholic beverages other than cider – became part of the staple diet.

Other modern amenities also reached the farmstead. The radio provided information about and links to the rest of the province and, indeed, the rest of the country. Convenient and affordable means of transport such as the bicycle and later the motorcycle allowed for increased mobility. A major consequence of the revolution in wants was that the *baserria* had to pay for the new utilities and goods in money. While most of the *baserriak* continued to follow subsistence patterns during the period in question (1925–45), they increasingly began to look to the market as both buyers and sellers. In the words of Douglass, 'the trend toward involvement in the marketplace was clear-cut and irreversible' (97).

In relation to changes in the household, the third period (1945–67) must be understood as a time of further advance and acceleration of the modernization process (98ff). *Baserri* operations became much closer linked to the market, which meant that money-dominated exchanges became even more important. Modernization and intensification of farming methods (modern fertilizing, silos, mechanized grass cutting) and a specialization and expansion in dairy farming and, additionally, poultry helped to generate extra cash income for the *baserria*. In Murelága cereal production and traditional shepherding were phased out. In Echalar cereal production also came to an end while sheep raising and farming continued to some extent but became less important than they once used to be. The most visible signs of change and the new economy were the pine forests in Murelága. By the mid-1950s the income from the pine forests had surpassed that derived from ordinary agriculture. A similar development could be observed now in Echalar where growing pines had less of a history than in Murelága but which, because of the potential benefits of the lumber industry in other parts of the Basque Country, now opted for planting pine trees. The result of that decision was a repetition of what Murelága had experienced a few years earlier, a conflict between sheep herding and the defenders of traditional *baserri* farming on one side and the new pine entrepreneurs on the other.

Other new features such as further changes in the staple diet were now omnipresent. Almost all bread was now bought; vegetables and fresh fruit became available in the stores, as was fresh fish. New forms of refrigeration and improvements in the transport sector made that change possible. The most notable changes related to the household infrastructure. Modern kitchens with gas cooking facilities replaced wood fires. Running water in the kitchen and in the bathroom was now available in almost all *baserriak*, improving sanitary conditions considerably. Communication and entertainment goods such as televisions, radios and telephones became even more widespread. These changes, together with other improvements in transport such as the ever-increasing use of motor vehicles, made the life of the *baserritarrak* clearly more convenient. All these new improvements also meant that the *etxekojauna* and his partner had to rely less on additional hands.

The modernization process also changed the setting. Douglass notes that around 1900 the village and its *baserriak* were still completely isolated, so isolated indeed that a large number of its inhabitants had never visited the provincial capital (109ff). Most interaction was still limited to regional markets, where valley traded with valley and village with village. Outside communication only happened through intermediate buyers. For most *baserritarrak* the *auzoa* was the most important space in terms of interaction and communication. The neighbourhood also remained the first port of call in terms of help.[37] Improved roads, and the use of motor vehicles and bus services in the period 1925–45, did not mean that *auzo* or village communication and solidarity were entirely replaced but they meant that they were no longer the closed and protected microcosmos they once used to be. Modern communication – radio, television and telephone – continued to connect the *baserritarrak* with the outside world.

37 As for Murelága, there also existed and continues to exist a town life with a church and a proper *plaza* at its centre, a *fronton*, a sports facility for playing the Basque ball game *pelota* and various bars and taverns, which the inhabitants of the *aldea* enjoyed. Town life in Echalar is considerably more limited. Two larger neighbouring towns, Lesaka and Vera de Bidasoa, serve as Echalar's administrative and recreational centres. Together with two other smaller towns they are know as the Cinco Villas.

Radical changes, such as in education, followed suit. Those born into a rural environment before 1930 were hardly able to read or write. Most if not all communication took place orally and in *Euskera*, the Basque language. With modernization also came regular schooling, especially reading and writing skills. In the rural environment of the Basque Country this also meant the arrival of the second language, Spanish. Most *baserritarrak* born after 1930 and schooled afterwards were now bilingual and had basic reading and writing skills. These important developments should not be underestimated for a variety of reasons, not least since most of the modernization came through the means of what was seen as an invasion and intrusion of Spanish into Basque culture. Some saw it as a victory of the former over the latter.

Summing up the developments, two specific local features can be noted. Murelága, although not necessarily in a better starting position, witnessed the exodus of some of its excess rural population, yet the town managed better than Echalar to create some work outside the *baserriak* environment. Lumber continued to flourish and became a major source for generating outside revenue for the local inhabitants. The marble-producing quarry that was part of the commonage also provided additional work and income for the surplus rural labour force. Additionally, two new small plants, both located in the centre of the village, one a shotgun factory and the other a fish processing plant, provided additional work. The nearby and rapidly developing industrial towns of Eibar and, to a lesser extent, Markina guaranteed that workers from Murelága could commute to work but still reside in the village or in the *baserria*. One could even speak of an emerging industrial sector in the village (120). In contrast, Echalar, which maintained its rural character in the context of the now omnipresent modernization process, could not provide its surplus rural population with anything comparable. Not even its geographical position close to the French border and the related contraband activities could stop the rural exodus of the younger generation of *baserritarrak*.

The problematic economic conditions such as the late and in many ways reluctant response to modernization led to an exodus to nearby metropolitan regions and larger industrial towns or to the New World. In the case of Echalar the rural exodus was notable in Irun, San Sebastián and its environs, and Pamplona. In the case of Murelága the next big towns of Eibar, Gernika and the metropolitan region of Bilbao were the destinations for the rural surplus population. The exodus was further complicated and partly accelerated by the events of the Spanish Civil War.[38]

The *baserria* had in many ways outlived its traditional function of providing for subsistence existence. It was no longer the self-sufficient unit it once had been. The accelerated modernization process and the rationalization of farming no longer demanded the traditional two-generational or even three-generational family. In the first instance, at the beginning of the modernization process, the *baserria* could resort to more intensive farming, animal husbandry and more intensive milk production. But this only worked for some time. Exploitation of the small landholdings including the already reduced commons could not provide adequately to the ever more dynamic market. By the late 1960s a limit to what could be achieved economically with a small farmstead had been reached. In the end, the traditional farmstead could not compete any more at a time when the industrialization of farming had become an omnipresent phenomenon and the commercialization of the countryside had made huge progress in other parts of the country.[39] Particularly devastating was the fact that land, which for the traditional *baserria* had a deeper cultural and social meaning, something beyond mere economics reasons, had been turned into a commodity. Once the process of modernization had reached the Basque rural world there was no turning back. More and more people sought a future in industrial employment or in emigration – or both. First there were just a few individuals; later more and more *baserritarrak* had to give up farming for part-time or full-time employment because the income derived from the farmstead simply would not suffice. Most Basque peasants who had once experienced the non-pecuniary life, work, and culture of the *baserria*

38 Douglass also notes different emigration patterns between Echalar and Murelága (120ff). Most Echalar emigrants leave never to return. Murelága knows very different patterns. It is common for the emigrant to return and to show that he has become a successful man abroad by investing again in his hometown and *baserri*.

39 The startling take-off and success of the southern parts of Navarre and the Rioja region would be a particularly good example in point.

as freedom now became part of a new salary and money-dependent culture (Douglass 1970/2003, 38f). Now it was not only the surplus rural population like unmarried siblings who had to leave the *baserria*, but increasingly the 'Lord of the House', his wife and their descendants.

On top of those objective conditions came challenges and changes that relate to more subjective dimensions, such as the cultural and social revolution in terms of wants and needs. No longer could the *baserria* be seen as a bulwark against such new influences. Modernization had undoubted advantages, from electricity and running water to other changes such as radio, the cinema, television and the new means of transportation. Who would want, under such new conditions, to inherit Basque-style and become a new *etxekojaun* or *extekoandre* with all its obligations?[40] What was once a promising and honourable role had, under modern conditions, become a life of diminished expectations and a danger to one's life chances – in short, a social and economic burden.

As to the further development of the Basque *baserria*, reliable data, because of the lack of official information, are hard to come by. The first agrarian census was carried out as late as 1962, with a second census following in 1972. Regrettably, most of the census questions were not specific enough to allow for a proper *baserriak* count. According to Miren Etxezaretta, who has tried to give a more detailed picture in her study *El caserío vasco* (1977), the census counted too many small units (anything above the size of 0.1 hectare qualified for being listed: altogether 36,232 agrarian units were counted) (122). Taking into account the fact that anything below two hectares is not big enough to qualify as a *baserri* and thus needs to be eliminated from the calculation, Etxezarreta's own estimate for the year 1973 is that roughly 17,500 *baserriak* existed in the two provinces Gipuzkoa (8,000) and Bizkaia (9,500) (124). She also notes that when the first census from 1962 is re-interpreted the same way and compared to the one

40 In his funeral rites study (1970/2003, 40) Douglass explains the early exodus in Murelága mainly by Basque inheritance patterns. Since the eldest son inherits the entire *baserria*, there is a structural exit model built into traditional custom; all other siblings will be forced out unless they submit to the new *etxekojauna*'s authority.

of 1972, it becomes obvious that the number of farmsteads was in steep decline and that the traditional *baserria* was obviously in crisis.

Although Etxezaretta's model is still very much based on the ideal model of the tri-generational family residing in the farmstead, she speaks of the *baserria*'s functioning and the related division of labour already in more dramatic terms than Douglass. We can safely assume that this difference is one based on an already different reality than the one Douglass encountered. In Etxezarreta's account four threatening tendencies are identified (130ff). First of all, in the modern *baserria* not all residents are involved in farm work. Some of the *etxekoak* have taken up part or full-time employment in industry. This applies particularly to the younger generation. The remaining, reduced farm work is divided up between family members or is done in extra time or part time. Second, although the Basque provinces actually witnessed an overall growth in population, the rural exodus to which Douglass had already alluded had become even stronger and was particularly noticeable in small rural towns. In the decade from 1960 to 1970 between 11.5 percent and 15.5 percent (an average of 14.4 percent) of the rural population had left to find employment somewhere else. The third tendency was that of urbanization and the migration of the rural surplus population into urban areas, in particular greater Bilbao.[41] The fourth trend, which can be described as the 'emptying and greying' of the *baserria*, was partly a result of and partly the driving force behind the rural exodus. Not enough hands were available to keep the traditional *baserria* afloat and not enough young people found *baserri* life attractive enough to stay. Those who stayed were mainly of the older generation. Out of the estimated 17,500 farmsteads in Gipuzkoa and Bizkaia, roughly 7,500 were taken care of by older people. More than a third of all Bizkaian *baserriak* had no family succession. As a result, where the typical traditional farmstead worked before with six or seven pairs of hands, there were now considerably

41 In rapidly developing industrial towns such as Eibar, Ermua or Hernani and in the metropolitan area of greater Bilbao the Basque rural exodus was joined by many emigrants who came from other parts of rural Spain, particularly from Galicia, Extremadura and Andalucía.

fewer (three to five people). While it is true that some of the farm work has become mechanized and some of the infrastructure modernized, it is also true that keeping an average four to ten hectare-size *baserri* afloat with so few, amounts almost to an impossible task.

As a response to the apparent difficulties, farmsteads have diversified and the traditional *baserria* is now just one type of farm amongst others. Etxezarreta lists the four main types: the traditional *baserria* that underwent some modernization in order to survive; the modern farmstead which represents a complete break with tradition and which is experimenting with new farming methods and products; modern farm enterprises, in essence small industries, that are dedicated to agricultural production and work; and finally, modern co-operatives which are no longer family-based or tri-generational (160ff). With such variety, rural life certainly continues to exist; however, it is no longer of the traditional order. The rural village has been, in effect, the great loser. As a matter of fact, the rural village and small town are now hardly recognizable as such. They intersect and interact now constantly with the urban environment and the industrial zones and developments that seem to be ever expanding and are increasingly invading what was formerly rural space. The radical change is also noticeable in terms of a changed cultural environment in which Spanish culture and language are seen as trying to dominate. For the remaining rural Basque population, modernization is mainly experienced as something imposed and as something that is not 'from here', but comes from outside – in other words, from 'Madrid'.[42]

42 How such cultural predispositions and perceptions can turn into violence is described by Joseba Zulaika in his study *Basque Violence: Metaphor and Sacrament* (1988). It tells the story of Itziar, a small rural town in Gipuzkoa that pertains administratively to Deba now, that underwent radical modernization with some industrial developments which can only be described as brutal. The industrialization process challenged the local traditional rural life and in the course of the 1970s led to the formation of a local ETA cell. During the course of the events described by Zulaika, people who once worked the same farm or were neighbours were now set against each other. People perceived as modernizers or supporters of change became agents of the Spanish state while ETA supporters claimed to represent true Basque (and traditional rural) values.

At the same time the traditional rural way is running out of alternatives; the remaining *baserritarrak* know that not to modernize would be the end for the *baserria* and the way of life it symbolizes. While various attempts at squaring the circle, partly by introducing new activities such as chicken and pig farming, increased meat and milk production, partly by forming *baserri* co-operatives, have been made (269ff and 333ff) the future remains unclear. Most of the alternatives require larger farmsteads with fewer personnel (farms below fifteen hectares barely merit the effort), additional technological resources and, above all, major capital investment. Even by the late 1970s the outcome of such modernizing efforts and models was predictable and was poignantly described by Etxezurreta: historical experience shows that it is almost unheard of for five poor peasants to turn into one rich farmer (333).[43]

2.3 Reluctant Modernization I: The *Baserria* as an 'Exit' Model of Moral Economy

E. P. Thompson has described the unique class constellation found in eighteenth-century England, just before capitalism's triumph (Thompson 1980, 260ff). What the historian finds, according to Thompson, is not the existence of a prototype or an otherwise easily identifiable industrial working or middle class. Instead, he suggests, we encounter a constellation consisting of a small oligarchic gentry and a numerically larger rural

43 The situation in rural Alava is somewhat different when compared to the coast. As Martínez Montoya (2002) has convincingly shown, the rural world of Alava has been, against all odds, well capable of responding to change by re-defining the relationship between the rural world (field/soil) and the urban world (town/city) and by maintaining its cultural symbols through modernizing rituals and practices. Martínez Montoya calls this process 'the new sacralization' of rural spaces. Whether this successful form of modernization is exportable to other Basque regions remains to be seen.

and small town plebs. Latent conflict and occasional open confrontation existed between the two but this was always mediated by the existence and occasional political and social intervention of the lower 'whiggish' gentry, the press, an insistence on rights, and by the occasional and almost always spontaneous local protest movements that could sometimes bridge social differences and mobilize people – from the poor to the lower gentry. Thompson points out that most of the craftsmen and traders who made up the small town and rural plebs had what can be called a rather 'vertical' and more individualistic consciousness in the sense of a high esteem or pride in their particular trade or craft. He contrasts this with the modern, more 'horizontal' collective notion of consciousness that one can encounter when studying modern industrial working class behaviour. However, the existence of a 'vertical' consciousness should not make us conclude that the plebs were under the total spell of the patrician land-owning elite or that they followed every order from above without questioning. In contrast, particularly when it came to defending traditional rights and customs, latent disquietude and dissatisfaction could easily lead to massive, often spontaneous protest and reactions (262).

Referring to these historical examples, Thompson addresses the larger question of whether historians and social scientists are actually sufficiently equipped and conceptually prepared for detecting a more complex notion of class, particularly when it comes to studying pre-industrial times and transitional periods. More specifically, and directed against a somewhat lifeless sociology, Thompson rejects a static notion of class. In defiance of the aridity of sociological and statistical surveys he proposes taking a closer look at local and regional historical varieties. Such a paradigm change would also allow the researcher to address unique conditions without easily assuming or proscribing the validity of one-size-fits-all, ahistorical class models.

Thompson argues further that it is wrong to re-read or re-project contemporary and modern notions of class struggle back into pre-industrial times. He suggests instead paying more attention to what the multitude of the plebs actually did, particularly in relation and reaction to the hegemonic class in power. Labelling such conflicts 'class struggle without class', Thompson observes that in the historical process, forms of collective consciousness usually come about at the end of the struggle. In other words, collective consciousness is the result of a struggle not its starting point. Class is about how people experience their condition and how they react when the social equilibrium is being threatened. Class consciousness can only be a result of this – not a precondition. Thompson has applied these conceptual insights to his own research into pre-capitalist class conditions and constellations. What the historian encounters when working with a different set of historical concepts can be described as an attempt to maintain an equilibrium where each condition of society must take account of the other. While the patrician gentry and oligarchy acted in a paternalistic way and expected to be followed, the plebs in turn demanded to be treated with respect (270ff). One must not imagine this constellation as an open confrontational conflict or struggle but rather as two gravitational fields trying to maintain an equilibrium. Despite such striving for balance, challenges were common enough and on occasion gave way to a more demanding and urgent pattern.

If the situation was as described, it should not come as a complete surprise that during a period of transition in the later eighteenth century, the societal equilibrium came under more and more pressure. This was mainly due to the rise of a new market economy that clashed with an older sense and practice of moral economy. The old moral economy, rich in its traditional symbolic values, was, according to Thompson, a unique expression of plebeian culture. Thompson suggests looking particularly at symbolic rituals and notions, such as the pride of being a freeborn Englishman (281). Such 'natural' notions of identity with their implicit calls for equality, justice and fairness help to explain the struggles for symbolic authority. Conflicts over common rights and traditional customs were always conflicts over hard-won entitlements. To understand them is crucial because it helps the historian or social scientist to conceive of the nature of patrician hegemony and power not as being total but rather as resembling an unwritten preliminary contract, which the plebs could always call into question when the equilibrium threatened to become destabilized and tip towards the side of the patrician oligarchy.[44]

Using mainly historical anthropological material and ethnographic sources, Thompson has also investigated such important locations as behaviour in pre-industrial and pre-capitalist market places. He argues that it is mainly in this context that a moral economy can be fully investigated. In his essay on moral economy and the English crowd, Thompson notes that the old economy – that is, the economy before capitalism's victory – still knew certain moral rules and regulations (Thompson 1980, 80ff). Developed from traditional subsistence production, the products of the farm or the sea were exchanged in direct face-to-face interaction and exchanged in local or regional markets. Everybody still knew each other; trade was the shortest way possible between producer and buyer and did not involve any intermediaries. There was no chain of trade to speak of. If one purchased from Farmer X (or Fishing Crew X), one usually knew what to expect and what the quality of the product was, who produced it and how it got to the market. The purchasing price was usually seen as just or fair in the sense that the buyer thought that the product was worth the amount of labour for which he paid. Additionally, production and consumption in the same small town, village or region led to a certain confidence or trustworthiness. Beyond that, the market place also became a scene for interaction and transaction of a more general type where news made the rounds and conversations took place. It was a meeting place where goods were traded or sold and it was a truly 'universal' experience in its own right.

44 With reference to the workings of an older moral economy, Thompson also points out that it is impossible to talk about economy and production without talking about culture and what Marx has called the social relations of production. It is indeed remarkable, argues Thompson, that while anthropology, folklore and social or regional history pay much attention to such details as customs in common, the critique of political economy has fallen behind in only seeing those expressions as secondary 'software', derived from an assumed economic 'hard drive'. With their attention to detail, such dedication usually meant that anthropologists, ethnographers, folklorists and local and social historians paint a much more pluralistic society than political economists, particularly when it comes to pre-industrial times or transitional periods such as those preceding modern capitalist relations (311).

It was universal in the sense that the crowd acquired a sense of its own multitude, size and power, as can be demonstrated by studying the early collective protests against rising bread prices, which the authorities often arbitrarily introduced without any prior warning, or sometimes without having consulted the direct producers or buyers (128). In contrast to the older moral economy, the universalizing trend of modern capitalist market conditions and trade are more anonymous in character and normally do not allow for such direct chains of interaction and notions of worthiness and fair exchange.

Reflecting on his own experiences within British Marxism, Thompson points out that the writing of history all too often implies working with two ideal type models only – the fully developed capitalist market and its non-industrial, non-capitalist predecessor. According to Thompson, this does the complexity of historical processes and particularly complex transitional periods little or no justice. Having investigated the conditions before capitalism's victory in England, Thompson concludes that what the historian can actually witness in the transitional period in question is a situation where the end of a tradition has been reached but where a new tradition has not yet emerged (121). He contends that it would be a violation of the available historical evidence if such a period were to be investigated with 'imperialistic' notions of two common and often-used ideal types, the non-developed pre-industrial model and the fully developed capitalist system. Instead, he suggests that it is through less rigid concepts such as plebeian culture and moral economy that the wealth of history in the making can be fully appreciated and understood.[45]

45 Plebeian culture does not, as already mentioned briefly above, refer to a rigid and elaborated class structure. Its moral impetus strives for a balance ('balance' or 'equilibrium' meaning here simply making enough for a living while respecting common customs and traditions as they have developed almost organically). 'Reciprocity', 'mutual obligation' and 'solidarity' are the keywords here (63 and 343). Using such concepts, Thompson is referring to a moral economy that does not know yet the full rationalization of modern, pecuniary culture in which the sense of production for profit becomes the only motive and begins to dominate all market exchanges. However, moral economy cannot be described as being necessarily revolutionary or

While E. P. Thompson's account provides many productive insights, it is also limited when applied to our context. While it is right to stress the processual dimension of complex class constellations such as the constant power play between plebeian culture and patrician gentry, there are also micro-institutional dimensions that need to be addressed. Thompson has always been more interested in the process and the occasional, often spontaneous, manifestations of class consciousness. In his account of plebeian culture and moral economy there is always a lot of uncharted territory and constant conflict in the way in which traditional rituals and common rights are ascertained. Surprisingly little is said about the rather sluggish nature of plebeian institutions other than the market place. Thompson also leaves open the question whether independent farmers played a significant part in the plebeian struggle. Particularly in small towns where those farmers usually sell their products and became part of the small town social network, they must have played a significant part in the plebeian struggle and its moral economy.

It is my contention here that Albert O. Hirschman's suggestions for studying aspects of moral economy, and particularly its institutional dimensions, by looking at various available options such as exit, voice and loyalty, provide an additional and useful element and help partly to explain what sometimes remains a black box in Thompson's view of moral economy.[46] It seems to me that in particular the exit option that Hirschman describes

---

proto-revolutionary either, although conflict situations were not uncommon. The historian is here referring to a plebeian culture which knew what practical solidarity meant but which did not express it 'horizontally' as classes do in modern times. According to Thompson's own poignant description, it is perfectly possible that in such transitional times we often encounter what seem to be contradictory elements. Thompson argues that we should acknowledge such complexity and weave it into our historical narratives. In a time where people expressed a common plebeian heritage, particularly at times when the social equilibrium was threatened, they 'were consumers also of cultural values, of libertarian rhetoric, of patriotic and xenophobic prejudice; and on these issues they could exhibit solidarities as well' (63).

46 For a more general overview of Hirschman's contribution to the critique of political economy see Hess (1999). I should add here that Hirschman has repeatedly addressed the question of agriculture and the rural countryside, particularly in his writings on

is of particular relevance to the analysis of the *baserria* crisis. In *Exit, Voice and Loyalty* Hirschman has described the three options that individuals have in relation to economic, political or social institutions. 'Voice' stands for protest or speaking out; literally it means voicing one's discontent. Only if the voice option has become exhausted, either because it is simply disregarded, not heard, or otherwise unsuccessful, does the 'exit' option of leaving appear as a radical alternative. 'Loyalty' links the two together and describes the ideal situation: loyalty is maintained if it allows for voice to be heard while at the same time keeping exit at bay. In his study Hirschman repeatedly pointed out that there are institutions where 'exit' becomes painful simply because membership is of a different nature or category.

It seems that with the *baserria* we are encountering exactly such a situation. Within families and even extended families the exit option will always be a tough choice – not only for the ones who have to leave but also for those who will be left behind. But with the primogeniture solution we not only encounter structural conditions for exit, we also encounter a slightly different formula from the one that Hirschman described as necessary for an equilibrium (where loyalty keeps exit at bay and allows voice to be heard). For the functioning and future survival of the *baserria* it is necessary to reformulate the Hirschmanian ideal scenario. It is now 'exit' that has become a sign of loyalty; 'voice' becomes – at least for the time being – structurally repressed or quelled. It may only ever come to light again once the constellation has changed entirely (in the sense that the exiled or the leaver opts for another life in another country or in a more urban environment where the person finds itself in a more 'voice'-friendly environment; or in the case where the entire *baserria* environment is threatened or perceived to be threatened – a situation where all *baserritarrak* may voice their discontent).

I mentioned in the introduction that E. P. Thompson's and Albert O. Hirschman's descriptions can, if modified, be productively applied to the Basque situation. It is particularly with reference to the history and

---

economic progress and Latin American development. However, in his writings on moral economy (Hirschman 1970 and 1977) very little is said about rural aspects.

function of the *baserria* as an institution that we can now try to put the ideas of the existence of a plebeian culture and moral economy to use and see the survival struggle of the *baserria* in a different light.

Taking at first a broad view and seeing the Basque *baserria* in a more general and European context, during transitional periods from medieval to modern times, the available historical material referred to in the previous sub-chapters shows that, in comparison, the rural Basque *baserritarra* and his farmstead stand out in terms of being relatively free from personal dependencies or other forms of direct interference and control. While rural folk and peasants of other countries and regions were serfs and suffered from complete personal dependency while working soil they did not own, the same cannot be said for the Basque case. I am not referring here to a rare exceptional decade or a century but I am pointing to an exceptionally long time period, ranging from the beginning of the sixteenth century to the end of the nineteenth century.

To be sure, there were considerable regional differences within the Basque Country; there were also numerous changes in the political structures until the Basque provinces emerged in their modern form. There were, particularly in pre-modern times, periods of great insecurity such as bandit wars. Also, the countryside saw conflicts about power and control in which the rural population and small-town plebs played a considerable part in providing a counterbalance to the *jauntxoak* and the political oligarchy in power. There were shortages that threatened the livelihood of the rural population and there were disasters such as the plague, which were more threatening in urban areas and towns but which had also an impact on the countryside. Finally, the Basque provinces have been subject to wars and foreign invasions.

Having briefly mentioned the political, social and sometimes natural intervening forces and constraints, it is safe to say that for a time period of almost three hundred years the Basque *baserria* and its occupants could develop in an almost organic fashion and were, again comparatively speaking, relatively free from direct dependencies or forms of direct oppression. More specifically, it is during this long period that the notion of Basque nobility became the accepted common view. It may well be the case that notions of egalitarianism also helped the 'patrician' oligarchy and the *jauntxoak* in their attempt to gain either access to or stay in power, or to benefit from being close to power. Bearing this in mind there is also another, plebeian side to the story. The conflicts of the nineteenth century between the new regime of mainly urban liberals and rural *carlistas*, who tried to maintain the *fueros* and the old order, and the support that the latter received from the rural countryside and the *baserritarrak*, demonstrates that the sense of tradition in combination with a sense of egalitarianism may have been more widespread and firmly established than some historians and social scientists are willing to accept.

Similarities between a notion of being a noble Basque and Thompson's notion of the 'freeborn Englishman' can easily be detected. As in the case of the English 'crowd' or plebs, the Basque case was also not free of contradictions. In the case of the *baserria* they were obvious: the *baserria* as an institution provided first and foremost for its occupants. It did so through heavy demands on the individuals who occupied the *baserria*. Hard labour and usually submission to the control of the *etxekojauna* are the very preconditions of its proper functioning. The way in which control and power of the *baserria* were maintained must also be seen as highly contentious. It depended in most cases on primogeniture, the passing on of the *baserria* to the eldest son. As we have seen, there were exceptions to the rule but even those exceptions were usually based on the exit of siblings. There was a reason for following this primogeniture model. Having only access to four to six hectares on average, it was necessary not to fragment the landholdings. The only way of doing so was not to break up the land and the *baserria*. But as we have also seen, the individual price that was paid was enormous; many people emigrated and sought their luck in the Americas or elsewhere; military or naval services were also options, as were the religious orders. With increased urbanization and industrialization other exit models became important such as leaving and looking for employment in the city or the next new industrial town.

Such exits allowed the traditional *baserria* to survive for a very long time before finally the arrival of modern industry and urbanization limited the survival perspectives of the *baserria* itself. The reluctant response to modernization and the new markets – actually supported as late as the 1920s by unrepentant nationalists including academics – put so much pressure on the *baserriak* that they could not survive in their traditional form. It was almost as if the traditional *baserria* was living on borrowed time. The call for historic rights and the old, independent institutions, first during the two Carlist wars, then later in the form of twentieth century nationalist claims, seemed almost to provide an ideological compensation for non-existing practical solutions.

If all of this sounds too negative, one must also see what the *baserria* and its occupants had to lose. As distinct from other countries the subsistence model of the *baserria* provided for its occupants and, even beyond, for the rural town or village (until the demographic changes and the growth of towns and cities shifted the demand side beyond what the *baserria* could provide). The form of practical help and solidarity that one could expect from the *auzoa* even took on an organized solidary form, as we have seen in Douglass's description. Furthermore, the Church in the Basque Country appears not, at least in the countryside and in the *auzoak*, to have been an oppressive force. It had rather become an institution which provided practical help through local parish and community contacts (almost in a bottom-up fashion through collective action and mutual help within the *auzoa*), relevant knowledge (more than once religious organizations suggested practical reforms) and even political representation (the rural *anteiglesias* of the valleys and the numerous brotherhoods that were formed are the prime examples that come to mind here). Free of oppressive landlords and masters, the *baserritarrak* were, comparatively speaking, living in satisfactory conditions. There was no hunger or malnutrition and people did not work as slaves but owned their land in most cases. In many ways the plebeian exit model of moral economy had a price – but it also worked. The traditional *baserria* and the moral economy it represented worked as long as the plebeian culture with its small towns and rural environment functioned. Once the settings began to change it fell behind. Even as early as the third decade of the nineteenth century the traditional *baserria* fell into crisis. Limited land holdings with little hope of expansion (including the commons) simply did not suffice and were not made for catering to an always expanding and demanding modern market.

That the *baserria* actually survived for another hundred years is due to compromise and concession (employing more intensive farming methods, changing the produce, and so on) but even this long survival struggle is a miracle and can only be explained by its cultural embeddedness, such as a strong sense of community and belonging. That culture was rural, small-town based, religious, proud to be Basque, oral and mainly *Euskera*-speaking, proud of an egalitarian ethos and free (whether it always delivered fully on the last two promises is, as we have seen, indeed questionable). The *baserria* and the culture it represented are in many ways illustrations of Thompson's plebeian culture and moral economy. It differed from the English model in that it seemed even more embedded, sharing perhaps significant more peculiar customs in common than did the British communities that Thompson referred to in his historical account. The *baserria* as an institution was also for a very long time successful because it was based structurally on the exit of large numbers of people. While all this sounds like a huge contradiction, it should be stressed here, first, that societal reality is full of contradictions and always more complex than the theory about it. It is, second, also important to bear in mind that Europe knows very few examples of places where its peasants or farmers were actually free for long periods of time. In relation to Albert O. Hirschman's discussion, I want finally to suggest here that the traditional *baserria*, its functioning and even its demise, can best be understood as representing a certain *modus vivendi* within plebeian culture. I suggest calling this the 'exit model of moral economy'.

CHAPTER 3

'Working the Waves': The Brotherhood of Fishermen and Moral Economy

Traditional rural institutions like the *baserria* are defined by their fixed character; they are truly embedded in their natural environment, surrounded by or in very close proximity to the land and those animals from which the produce of the farmstead is generated. Through interaction with its immediate surrounding, *baserria* culture creates its own rich world and references. Yet this rich experience was not necessarily always functional when it came to dealing with the outside world. As we will see – and this is very much in contrast to *baserria* culture – the relationship the Basques have with the sea points towards a very different set of values and relations, in which local conservationism and customs have had to find answers to questions such as the principle of universal accessibility to the sea and the challenge of changing conditions, particularly when faced with competition in an international market. Thus, the story of the Basques and their relationship with the sea can be described as a continuous struggle between 'closure' and occasionally strong protectionist measures on the one hand, and equal access and adjustment to open markets on the other. Furthermore, this struggle can also be interpreted as a struggle for representation and as an attempt to make the voice of fishermen heard. At the centre of this struggle is an institution known as the *cofradía*. How successful this institution has been in providing representation – taking into account also the different functions the *cofradía* has had in its long history as an institution – is a point of ongoing debate. Before these questions can be addressed it is necessary to outline how over the centuries the Basques have dealt with the challenges and opportunities of facing the Atlantic Ocean in general and the Bay of Biscay in particular.

3.1 The Sea and the Harbour: A Short History of the *Cofradía*

The first mention of the existence of a landmark along the Basque coast, the Cape of Higuer, is in the sixth century BC and stems from a Greek source, Avienus from Marseilles.[1] The second mention comes again from a Greek source, Pytheas, who gave a first description of the Iberian coastline in 330 BC. More detailed evidence can be found in the second century AD: Claudius Ptolemy was the first to identify specific landing places, such as the mouth of the Nervión river and the river Deva and a number of other smaller settlements. The next description appeared in the fourth century when the Roman writer Marcianus of Heraclea listed details of and distances between various settlements, rivers, capes and ports. However, specific references to Aquitaine and what is today the southwest coast of France and the Cantabrian coast are few.

The Romans of the late Empire were the first to chart properly the contours of the Bay of Biscay, or the *oceanus cantabricus* as Orosius and Claudius called it. It was also during the late Roman Empire that a small naval base was established at the mouth of the river Bidasoa.[2] Rome never fully penetrated and conquered the area (which today forms the Basque province of Gipuzkoa) or the territories which lie even further west such as Bizkaia. For strategic reasons Rome was more interested in establishing a firm base in the province of *Lapurdum* (today the region around Bayonne), where she erected a military fort that also became a major trading point.

By the early medieval period regular trade between the northwest of Spain (today's Galicia) and the southwest of France was firmly established. Such trade routes required harbours and proper stop-over possibilities in between. At that time orientation and navigation were possible only by

1 Here and in the next paragraphs I follow the accounts of Baroja (1985, 14ff) and Ciriquiain Gaiztarro (1986, 12ff).

2 In modern times the river has become the natural border, which separates the French part of the Basque Country (Iparralde) from the Spanish part (Hegoalde).

identifying capes and important landmarks along the coast and by sailing from port to port. More sophisticated navigation arrived with the Vikings who, after having explored the northwestern parts of Europe, also took an interest in the wealthy ports of the south-west Atlantic coast of France. Bayonne in particular seems to have been subject to Viking raids in the eleventh century. Despite their frequent raids, the Vikings did not make any systematic efforts to settle or to colonize the region.

For the period between the eleventh and fourteenth centuries detailed information is hard to come by but piracy seems to have been a not uncommon way of making a living along the Biscayan coast. Pirates mainly hunted on Bayonne's established trade routes, which by the end of this period involved the entire coast from Portugal to Bayonne.[3] In the thirteenth and fourteenth centuries in particular a major effort seems to have been made to develop and integrate every accessible port along the Cantabrian coast. The founding of San Sebastián was followed by royal charters for Fuentarrabía, Oyarzun, Getaria, Motrico, Zarautz, Zumaia, Orio and Usurbil. A second wave of foundations which received royal recognition included the Bizkaian ports of Ondarroa, Lekeitio, Mundaka, Bermeo, Plentzia and various smaller ports located at the mouth of the Nervión river (or what today constitutes greater Bilbao). Official agreements were common, such as the one in the early fourteenth century between Bayonne and a number of ports in Bizkaia, Gipuzkoa and Cantabrico which regulated their respective trade with Portugal.

At the beginning of the sixteenth century the infrastructure was so well developed that even remote inland regions such as Alava and Castile had become an integral part of the network. Technological advances in shipbuilding together with improved trade and communication led to accelerated growth, which in turn led to the development of early forms of urban architecture in the otherwise small harbour towns of Gipuzkoa and

3 It is important to distinguish the earlier *itsaslapurra* (pirate or *ladrón de mar*) from the later appearance of the commissioned and semi-legal *corsura joan* or *ibilli* (corsair) (Baroja 1985, 41ff).

Bizkaia.[4] Within Bizkaia, Bilbao and Bermeo developed into the busiest ports. Yet cities outside the Basque Country like Seville and later Cadiz also profited from Basque knowledge of shipbuilding and seafaring. The three most famous examples are the combined expedition to the Canary Islands (1398) in which Gipuzkoa, Bizkaia and Seville participated, the voyages of Christopher Columbus in which numerous Basque mariners took part, and the success of the Basque captain Elcano from Getaria who, together with thirty-four other Basque seamen, managed to complete Magellan's pioneering project of circumnavigating the globe after the death of the leader of the expedition.

In addition to the development of trade (and its dependant, piracy) one should not neglect the history of other significant parallel developments and activities such as fishing and whale hunting. Earlier, both fishing and whale hunting had been limited to coastal waters. Coastal fishing for *besugo* (bream), *merluza* (hake), *sardina* (sardine), *antxoa* (anchovies) and *bonito* (white tuna) had a long-established tradition, reaching as far back as the earliest human settlements along the Basque coast. Some Basque words that are related to the sea, such as *itxaso* (sea), *arrantzale* (fisherman) or *arrain* (fish), show no etymological links with any other language, which indicates that these activities must have been in existence for a long time (Baroja 1985, 41).[5] Yet the hunting of whales needed more sophisticated technologies and purpose-built boats and vessels were introduced from

4 Most harbour towns along the Cantabrian coast are either situated in small access valleys or located at the mouth of a river. In both cases the surrounding mountainous landscape and the otherwise steep coastline do not allow for much horizontal development. A symbolic expression of the vertical architecture and urbanization process can still be seen in many harbour towns. Single-storey dwellings or single family homes rarely exist inside the old towns. Most houses have at least three floors. A particularly spectacular example can be seen in Motrico/Mutriku where the Torre de Berriatua, a mid-sixteenth-century five-storey building, survives to this day.

5 There are early documents which confirm that Basques had been hunting the *Balaena Biscayensis* from as early as the tenth century onwards (Thalamas Labandibar 1935, 85f).

the twelfth century onwards.[6] Basque ports such as Fuenterrabía, Bermeo, Getaria, Lekeitio, Motrico and Ondarroa became famous for their whale hunting techniques, and to this day show whale-hunting activities on their coat of arms. Over time the activity and profession of the *ballenero* (whaler) and the *tostarteko* (fisherman)[7] became distinct from the *marinero* (mariner or sailor). However, coastal whale hunting was still based on rowing. Not until the fourteenth century had the shipbuilding of whalers developed to such an extent that it permitted seafaring based on wind and sails and thus finally allowed for transatlantic journeys. Basque sailors managed to reach *Terranova* (Newfoundland) where they began to explore and exploit the rich sea banks and hunting grounds just off the American coast. Crucial to such substantial exhibitions were improved navigation and the development of methods and techniques for preserving and processing the catch. The success of preserving and transporting cod (*bacallu* in Euskera, *bacalao* in Spanish) through salting proved to be a particularly invaluable invention.[8] Whales were immediately processed, their blubber was turned into oil and other useful substances while the bones were used for tools. At first intermittently but later on a regular basis, whale hunting and cod fishing flourished for centuries before the rise of English sea power and the long-lasting conflict between Spain and England prevented Basque sailors from accessing Newfoundland waters as regularly as they had done before.

6 Early whaling in Bizkaia and Gipuzkoa followed a well-defined course of action. Once the whale had been spotted by the *atalyero* (from *atalaya*: watch tower; *atalyero*: the guard, or watchman) a boat was immediately launched. In the beginning the crew consisted of four people, three rowing, the fourth crew member, the harpooner, commanding and steering the boat. While invoking the Virgin of Itziar, the religious figure of the fishermen of the region, the harpooner tried to ram his harpoon into the whale. In the case that the whale was caught, the mammal would be towed into the harbour or launch pad where it was then processed.

7 *Tostarteko* literally means 'the man between the rowing seats', referring to the fact that in early coastal fishing and whaling, rowing boats were used to reach the particular zone where the fishing or whale hunting took place.

8 For more details see Mark Kurlansky's fascinating books *Cod* (1997) and *Salt* (2002).

As Julio Caro Baroja has pointed out, this was not the first time Basque fishermen had to decide which side to join. Over a long period, conflicts broke out between England and France on the one hand and between England, Navarre and Castile on the other – usually over successions to the crown – resulting in constantly shifting allegiances for the Basques. Furthermore, such conflicts could have very different implications depending on whether one was a fisherman, a mariner, a ship builder, or a trader, and whether economic activity depended on private or public initiative (Baroja 1985, 51). Often certain alliances that related to the sea found their equivalent expression on land, and occasionally vice versa; hence the numerous splits into factions and family feuds that makes the early medieval history of the Basque region so complex. Some of the tensions and feuds were overcome only by the later rise and formation of larger political units such as the Kingdom of Navarre and later the Kingdom of Castile and their respective *señorios.*[9]

The multiple demands of fishing, trade, discovery, conquest and war activities for purpose-built ships led to even more technological rationalization and advances in shipbuilding and navigation. Two influences were crucial in this respect, one Nordic, the other Mediterranean. The Basques were masters at bringing these two different traditions together. A wide range of qualifications and skills were needed for building and navigating the new Atlantic vessels; the spectrum of people employed ranged from pilot to seafaring instructors. In terms of construction the combination of wood and iron was also new.[10] As Baroja (2003, 243) has pointed out, in this respect the location and environment of the Cantabrian coast proved to

9 By this time the Basque coast seemed to have been fully mapped. In 1622, Texeira provided the most detailed description so far. Listed for all Gipuzkoan and Biskaian harbours are such important details as type of port entry, depth of the sea, harbour facilities and protection (Ciriquiain Gaiztarro 1986, 20).

10 The new Atlantic vessels could have a weight of up to 1,200 tons. They were usually built with the help of the formula 'tres, dos y as', referring to 30 *codos* for the length, 15 for the width and 5 for the height (and reaching 45 for the top mast) (Baroja 2003, 254f). Clearly the construction of such vessels was no longer possible in small artisan places; it was now time for proto-industrial *astilleros* and *fererías* to replace them.

be ideal: it had the ocean and water on one side and iron and wood on the other side. The success of Basque shipbuilding was such that Larramendi in his seminal work on Basque etymology could later identify a whole range of words that originally stemmed from other cultures but that had been assimilated into Basque: *galea*, *galera*, *cabela*, *goitala*, *chalupa* all referred to different types of purpose-built boats or vessels, while words like *muelle*, *caya* and *kai* were used to describe parts of the launching infrastructure (Baroja 1985, 54f). Whether it was whalers, vessels for the merchant marine or battle ships, for a long time the wharfs of the Basque ports and ports like Seville and Cadiz, which relied heavily on Basque knowledge and their international links and experience, took the lead in the development of and advancement in shipbuilding and navigation.[11]

The keywords 'knowledge' and 'international experience' should not come as a complete surprise here. At the beginning of the seventeenth century there was already a Basque diaspora, which could be relied upon and used for a variety of purposes. Its activities began with participation in the early Spanish conquest of Latin America and included military campaigns (as in the case of the infamous and ruthless campaigns of Lope de Aguirre in the quest for *Eldorado*) and religious indoctrination through the establishment of centres in the urban environment as was the case with the Franciscan order, or religious outposts in the form of Jesuit-dominated settlements (another movement which had its origins in the Basque Country). Later, the Basque presence in Latin America would develop into more civic oriented activities such as establishing trade points in South America (Venezuela and Argentina in particular) and contributing considerably to the development of shipbuilding and navigation.[12]

11 The Motrico-born constructor, engineer and architect Gaztañeta (1656–1728) was one of the outstanding and well-respected figures of that time. The hegemony of the Spanish empire and with it a number of influential Basque figures in it – such as Gaztañeta – only came to an end when challenged and surpassed by the British empire.

12 The most important activities were those of the Real Compañia Guipuzkoana de Caracas (founded 1728), which later helped to develop the Compañia de Filipinas

To benefit truly from diaspora contacts, more was needed than just the simple presence of a critical mass of people of the same origin in the same place. It was after all a network of local, regional and internationally operating institutions that proved to be the key factor for participating in the developing international market and for facilitating economic contact and exchange. Such institutions as the various *hermandades* (brotherhoods) and *consulados* (consulates) – the most important one being the *Consulado del Bilbao* – increasingly directed their efforts towards national and international trade and provided the support which gave the diaspora its extra socio-economic power.

With the former Spanish and Portuguese colonies gaining independence and the advancement of seafaring knowledge in other parts of Europe, particularly in Holland and England in the eighteenth century, the traditional Spanish approach to maintaining colonial relations suffered serious setbacks. By the nineteenth century Spanish naval power and the empire it had supported were truly consigned to the realms of history.[13] Yet the decline of Spanish military power was not accompanied by a parallel decline or even disappearance of merchant or fishing fleets. Industrial whale-hunting apart, fishing and trade survived the decline of Spanish naval power. In the course of the nineteenth century, and in particular in Bilbao, Bermeo and Pasaia, some exceptional advances were made in terms of modern shipbuilding. These advances were partly due to the increasing industrialization and integration of the hinterland. In the immediate environment of Bilbao this involved not only the rapidly growing coal and iron industry nearby, but also the integration of various smaller ports at the mouth of the Nervión, such as Portugalete and Santurtzi. In 1832, Bilbao saw the introduction of the first industrial furnace, indicating the further development and integration of the local metal and iron industry, an infrastructure which would help to revolutionize shipbuilding along

---

(founded 1780). For a detailed historical account of the activities of the Caracas Company see Hussey (1934).

13 The 'official' end came when the Spanish lost the Spanish–American war, with Cuba becoming independent.

the Cantabrian coast. In 1902, the *Altos Hornos de Bilbao* was established; its workings signaled another change – the arrival of big-style modern corporations in shipbuilding.

While such a beneficial infrastructure helped the Basque shipbuilding industry and also had an impact in terms of modernizing and internationalizing Bilbao's trade, fishing remained largely unaffected by such modernizing efforts, although the introduction of steam and the diesel engine had some impact. But more than these few technological advances, what stood out was the perseverance and maintenance of long-established local traditions and the professional national and international links that had helped to preserve the Basque fishing fleet for centuries. Although fishing had always existed, its unspectacular parallel life has somehow been obscured by 'big picture' views of history, which focus entirely on the rise and fall of empires and their fleets, as the Spanish example clearly demonstrates. An essential requirement for the maintenance of the Basque fishing fleet was, and still is, the existence and functioning of an institution known as the *cofradía* (confraternity). The *cofradía*'s local contribution, at least when compared to the great colonial trading tradition, might seem to be minor, but over the centuries it has turned out to be a crucial stabilizing factor in the lives of Basque fishing communities. The *cofradías* of the Basque fishing ports dealt mainly with the regulation of fishing activities and the landing and sale of fish. The latter activity must be understood not solely as a purely local activity but as one with consequences reaching far beyond it. It is to this complex mechanism of the functions and history of the *cofradías* that we now turn.

While fishermen fulfill an important function, their role in political history has been seen as negligible (Pascual 1997, 16ff). Land and the peasants who lived and worked on it have been portrayed as more significant, as the histories of Europe, Russia, Asia and Latin America suggest. The difference between fishermen and peasants or farmers can be explained by reference to the different media from which they extract their products. The sea and the fishing grounds do not form a stable object or environment; there are no bounded properties, at least not in the sense of anything close to the possibilities on land. Coastal exclusion zones, which are intended to keep foreign intruders out, may be better defined but they still do not guarantee a successful catch.[14] In short, when it comes to the sea as a medium, maintaining 'the field' has always been difficult. Furthermore, fishing can be described as an activity that is beyond the complete control of individual labour or effort. Until about a century ago (and depending on the type of fishing), it was an activity that shared more similarities with hunting than with industrialized modern labour. Constant observation is crucial: factors such as the different seasons, weather and wind, sea conditions, the capacity to direct the vessel to the exact fishing grounds, the migration patterns of the potential stock or species, the technology that is applied to actually catch the fish – all play a role.[15] It was not until the beginning of the twentieth century that fishing turned into a full-blown industrial and increasingly rationalized activity,[16] including the full separation of

14 The six-mile zone, which has now been extended into a 200-mile zone provides more stability but it is a fairly recent twentieth-century invention.

15 In the last few decades coastal fish farming seemed to have changed this. It is an activity which resembles that of working the soil. The fish-farmer is its main protagonist. However, as with the soil, the issue of property is crucial. Out on the sea the relevance and functioning of knowledge and property structures are much more complex.

16 For a detailed description of the changed nature of fishing see Iñaki Martin Bermejo's instructive article 'El pescador actual, la tecnología y la gestión de los recursos pesqueros: extrapolando el caso de Orio', in: Rubio Ardanaz (ed.) (2003) *La pesca y el mar: cambio sociocultural y económico* (Zainak, Special Issue), 59–93. Martin Bermejo argues that against the old concept of 'luck' and 'traditional ethos', as for example elaborated in Zulaika's study of Basque cod fishermen working off the coast of Newfoundland (Zulaika 1981). More specifically Martin Bermejo stresses that new technological means in communications (global positioning systems (GPS, plotters)), fishing techniques (new advancements in heat detection for example), refrigeration and modern shipbuilding together with modern financial services and support have revolutionized the modern fishing enterprise to such an extent that to speak of 'luck' and 'ethos' no longer captures the new reality of Basque fishermen. The author's critique peaks in the argument that today no *patrón* or *capitán* will invest half a million Euro or more for a new vessel without knowing that there will be a considerable return in profit. The guarantee for generating profit is of course the newly available technological means which reduce 'luck' and the question of 'traditional ethos' considerably if not totally. However, while Martin Bermejo is right in stressing the declining factor of luck and ethos, he somehow forgets that fishing does not always develop in a unilinear fashion. The Basque Country is, as we will see in the next sub-

capital and labour, resulting in social stratification and leading, in part, to the proletarianization of the work force.[17] Yet, proletarianization is not a universal condition or an inherent tendency amongst fishing communities. Its occasional occurrence depends on many factors and circumstances, particularly the type of fishing methods employed. In the Basque Country, to this day, traditional elements and customs have survived and still continue to play a role in fishing.[18] In short, fishing was and still remains a complex activity that does not present a uniform or one-dimensional picture.

Fishing has been described as a form of interaction between man and the environment (Baroja 2003, 244ff). The Cantabrian coast does not, with the exception of a few estuaries, provide easy access to the ocean. The Atlantic waters of the Biscayan Sea reach considerable depths, they are not easily navigable because stream and wind conditions do not follow the same directions and weather conditions change constantly. The Basque *homo faber* who occupied the *kostaldea* had therefore to be extremely considered and careful in his approach to the sea. It took centuries of effort and experience before the Basques managed to bring the different elements of the sea and the land – water, iron and wood – together, so that they provided man with the tools to extract more fish from the sea.

The first and most important step that allows for regular interaction between man and the environment, between the fisherman and the sea, is the existence of proper facilities for embarkation. In other words, the establishment of ports was the decisive step in the evolution of fishing, since it is the place where the communication systems of the sea and those of the

chapter, marked by a pluralism of fishing traditions and methods. One of its main characteristics is the co-existence of traditional and modern features – hence also some of the major conflicts that are dealt with later in the text.

17 Whaling is a completely different process and has been subject to industrial capital-labour relations since the beginning of the nineteenth century. Herman Melville's *Moby-Dick* describes this process in great detail. A very good interpretation of *Moby-Dick* in terms of describing the new forms of industrial labour under capitalism is C. L. R. James's *Mariners, Renegades and Castaways* (1978).

18 For more information on the social scientific study of fishermen and its possible applications to Basque conditions see Rubio-Ardanaz, J. A. (1994).

land meet.[19] It has already been pointed out that the Basque Coast offers very few such points of encounter. It should come as no surprise then that the first efforts to build and fortify landing places were focused on areas where navigable rivers ended in the sea and provided natural access. From east to west these *villas ribereñas* were Fuentarrabía, Orio, Deva, Lekeitio, Gernika/Mundaka and the settlements at the mouth of the river Nervión. Starting in the eleventh and stretching into the twelfth century, anchorage and simple launch facilities developed into proper ports, encouraged by what can be called a parallel take-off phase of two types of activities, whaling and coastal fishing (*pesca litoral* or *pesca de bajura*).[20] Soon other ports would follow and by the thirteenth and fourteenth centuries coastal fishing had developed to such an extent that Basque fishermen were encouraged to try their luck further afield. This type of fishing would become known as *pesca de altura* (high sea fishing).

By the sixteenth century fishing had become more difficult. While coastal fishing continued to be practiced on a smaller scale, coastal whale hunting had almost completely disappeared and was only practised, together with cod fishing, along the coast of Newfoundland.[21] Towards the end of

19 Here and in the following paragraphs I follow Ciriquiain Gaztarro's detailed history of ports in the Basque Country (1986, 36ff) and Erkoreka Gervasio's comprehensive study of *cofradías* in those same ports (1991).

20 Documents from Lekeitio, Getaria, Zarautz and Fuentarrabía (referred to in: Thalamas Labandibar, 1935) reveal the extent to which whale hunting had become a standard practice. Here are some of the figures: whales landed in Lekeitio per year: 1531: 1; 1532: 0; 1536: 3; 1538: 6; 1542: 4; 1543: 1 and 1545: 2. For Getaria the same source lists one whale every year between 1684 and 1698. For Hondarribia/Fuentarrabía the numbers are similar: 21 whales for the time period 1610–35, including five alone in 1631. In Zarautz 55 cataracts were counted in the course of the eighteenth century. It is reported that the Cofradía de Mareantes in Fuentarrabía had all the necessary infrastructure to process whales in the harbour. One can assume that a similar infrastructure was in place in most Gipuzkoan and Bizkaian harbours which were dedicated to the hunting of whales.

21 Thalamas Labandibar (1935, 87f) quotes from a source, a San Sebastián whaling company, which in 1625 counted 41 vessels, 248 *chalupas* and 1575 crew, clearly indicating that in the seventeenth century whaling in Newfoundland had become a big industry. Thalamas Landibar also notes that by the second half of the seventeenth century there

the sixteenth century crisis hit the Basque ports. The Spanish Armada and its campaigns put a heavy demand on the resources of the ports – both in terms of financial and human resources. Despite such constraints regular fishing expeditions continued, covering the entire area of the North Atlantic and obviously returning enough profit to cope even with the extraordinary demands made by the Armada.

The differentiation in fishing and its increasingly complex operations demanded an appropriate representation of interests and a functioning organization responsible for the ports. The oldest written documents that reveal the existence of such fishermen's organizations on the Basque coast, the *cofradías*, go as far back as the fourteenth century; however the documents are probably just the legitimation of an activity that is much older.[22] The influences which led to the institutionalization of *cofradías* were initially religious ones. In France the idea of a corporation for professions and jobs had already taken root and the news had made it to the Cantabrian coast through Santiago pilgrims and had also spread from nearby monastic orders. Yet the speed with which the new ideas were appreciated and set into practice hint also at the unique professional conditions of fishermen. Exposed to the sometimes brutal forces of nature and often restrained from working by seasonal circumstances that were beyond their control, the fishermen were naturally inclined to solidarity and mutual help and decided to join forces to minimize the risks that fishing and seafaring frequently involve.

The fishermen's organizations were supported in their effort by the Kingdom of Navarre, which equipped them with special rights (the *fueros*). The existence of *cofradías* initially raised the suspicion of the Kingdom of Navarre's conqueror, the Castilian monarchy. Representing only fishermen,

---

were more than 3,000 fishermen in embarkations whaling abroad. Similar numbers were involved in cod fishing. For the first half of the seventeenth century Thalamas Labandibar speaks of 30 vessels each with 33 to 40 crew on board.

22 Erkoreka Gervasio points out that in terms of professional associations similar developments could be observed in other parts of Europe. He mentions the Roman *collegia* and the German guilds. Most developed out of a need for mutual help and protection and had in one way a religious dimension in that they had been encouraged by the Church and her teaching (Erkoreka Gervasio 1991, 31).

the *cofradías* had originally not only an exclusive character but had also been granted certain judicial rights which conflicted with the exclusive authority and character of the Castilian authorities (Erkoreka Gervasio 1991, 35f; Urzaonqui, T. and De Olaizola, J. M. 1998, 167–252). Eventually, the two sides seem to have acknowledged each other; the *fueros* that had originally been granted were either renewed or followed by some other official recognition and authorization. This process included the ratification of the *ordenanzas* (statutes), often containing fiscal agreements and legal procedures, which the new authorities ceded to the *cofradía* and which the fishermen had to follow and enforce.[23] The statutes and rules continued to be refined throughout the fifteenth, sixteenth and seventeenth centuries. This process of amending the statutes was an attempt at continuous rationalization and an endeavour to find a balance, which often walked the thin line between solidary aspects and the maintenance of common traditions, while also responding to exterior pressures and market forces. Table 1 shows the main developments that took place in each Basque port up to the late eighteenth century.[24]

23 Erkoreka (1991, 35ff) raises some points of discussion that are of interest in this context, namely that such official acknowledgement and authorization from the Crown also applied to other medieval institutions such as universities. However, unlike universities, the acknowledgement of *cofradías* was probably not designed to last forever and over time there have been various attempts to close down or prohibit the fishermen's institution. The contradictory nature of official Castilian authorities was demonstrated by the fact that while some selected *cofradías* got royal confirmation (San Sebastián, Deva, Motrico, Lekeitio and Bermeo) others never did and thus operated in a lawless, unregulated context. It seems that the non-acknowledged *cofradías* were tolerated as long as they 'delivered' (i.e. paid) their contributions.

24 A more detailed account of the development of each *cofradía* in Hegoalde has been provided by Erkoreka Gervasio in his study *Análisis histórico–institucional de las cofradías de mareantes del País Vasco* (1991, 46ff). The great advantage of this study is that the appendix reproduces all historical documents that are related to the history of the Basque *cofradías* in what is today the Spanish part of the Basque Country, Hegoalde (1991, 441–664). The ports and *cofradías* of the French part of the Basque Country (Iparralde) have been excluded here because following the French Revolution all feudal institutions and associations which held special rights were disallowed and ceased to exist.

Table 1. Main developments of Basque ports and *cofradías* from the thirteenth to the nineteenth century. (The table only lists the ports of Hegoalde in geographical order from east to west.)

	First official titles of town ('Carta Puebla'), fuero granted or other offical documentation	*First mention or official acknowledgement of port; confirmed existence or cofradía or first written cofradía statutes ('Ordenanzas')*	*New or modified cofradía statutes; other signs of modernization or relevant port activities*
Fuentarrabía/ Hondarribia	1203: *fuero* Navarro granted to Irun and Hondarribia	1339: existence of *cofradía* confirmed	
Pasaia	1320: titles of town	1799: existence of *cofradía* mentioned	1740: home base of the Compañia de Caracas; 1778: home base of the Compañia de Filipinas; 1807: official *cofradía* statutes

---

Erkoreka's account of the history of the individual ports and *cofradias* relies in part on Ciriquiain-Gaiztarro's pioneering and detailed work on the history of Basque ports. (Ciriquiain-Gaiztarro 1986). I have also used this source and extracted some information from it in order to draw up Table 1. For additional information I have also consulted Urzainqui and De Olaizola's *La Navarra Marítima* (1998).

Erkoreka distinguishes between 'old' and 'new' *cofradías*, ordering them from east to west. It must be stressed in this context that the fact that historical documentation is missing or is not available does not necessarily mean that some ports were behind in their development or had difficulties adjusting. In some cases we must assume that early written documentation has simply been lost or has inadvertently been destroyed. Motrico, one of the oldest ports, is a good example. Founded in 1209 and acknowledged through the Royal Charter, it is listed as a 'new' *cofradía* although it is highly likely that a *cofradía* existed even before the town had received official recognition. Erkoreka acknowledges this dilemma himself, suggesting that it might be better to imagine the development of the different ports as a continuum rather than as two separate historical developments. It is worthwhile noting that the crucial period of founding harbour towns was an initiative of the Kingdom of Navarre. The Kingdom of Castile built on these efforts and extended the program of developing the port facilities along the Basque coast.

San Sebastián	1014: first mention; 1200: *fuero* granted	1489: Cofradía Santa Catalina; Cofradía de San Pedro	1539: statutes modified; 1642: statutes modified
Orio	1379: *fuero* de San Sebastián granted	1520: existence of *cofradía* first mentioned	
Zarautz	1237: *fuero* Navarro granted to San Sebastián	1465: existence of *cofradía* first mentioned	
Getaria	1201: confirmation of privileges; 1204: *fuero* of San Sebastián granted	1537: existence of *cofradía* first mentioned; 1658: written *cofradía* statutes	1738: construction of new port after the old pier has been damaged by storm; 1747: statutes modified; 1753 and 1783: storms damage infrastructure considerably; 1825: statutes modified again
Zumaia	1292: first mention; 1347: *fuero* Navarro de San Sebastián	1585: officially acknowledged as port; 1610: *cofradía* founded	1925: track and train connection between Zumarraga and Zumaya
Deba	1294: *fuero* of Vitoria granted; 1343: titles reconfirmed	1448: Cofradía de Mareantes de Deba and written statutes	
Motrico/ Mutriku	1209: titles of town	1599: Cofradía de Mareantes de San Pedro and written statutes	1815–31: *cofradía* owns the entire *muelle*
Ondarroa	1327: titles of town; Fuero Navarro de Logroño	1353: first mention of *cofradía*; 1593: first written *cofradía* statutes	1638: *cofradía* statutes modified; 1847–95: improvement to piers in the harbour; 1892–1932: canalization of river

Lekeitio	1325: titles of town; Fuero Navarro de Logroño	1334: officially acknowledged as port; 1485: royal confirmation; 1488: first written *cofradía* statutes	1766: statutes modified
Ea	1777: first mention of settlement	1884: acknowledgement as port	
Elantxobe	1783: construction of *muelle*; 1782: titles of town after separating from Ibarranguela	1850s: development of port	
Mundaka	1335: first mention	1606: development of port facilities; 1656: first mention of natural harbour; 1697: first mention of existence of *cofradía*; 1755: first written statutes	1833: statutes modified
Bermeo	1082: first mention; 1236: Fuero Navarro de Logroño 1269: titles of town known to exist	1352/53: Cofradía de Mareantes; 1353: written statutes 1503: existence of pier for disembarkation officially documented	1723: repair work to piers 1862–81: modernization of harbour infrastructure; 1866: statutes modified; existence of three ports: Puerto Chico, Puerto Mayor and Portuondo
Plentzia	1299: titles of town and Fuero Navarro de Logroño	1524: written statutes	1694: statutes modified; 1791: statutes modified; 1858: construction of harbour facilities
Algorta		1545: mention of port development and improvements	1785: full port facilities

Bilbao	1300: titles of town	1372: first maritime code granting Bilbao's port freedom and privileges 1511: guarantee of primacy over other ports of the Nervión river; with the founding of the Cofradía de Mareantes y Mercadores (later: Consulado de Bilbao), development of internationally operating merchant fleet; 1527: construction of improved port facilities	1658: construction of muelle in Deusto; 1712: existence of two access canals (one via Santurtzi and the other via Algorta)
Portugalete	1322: titles of town; Fuero Navarro de Logroño	1463: agreement between Portugalete and Bilbao ports; 1532: construction of new *muelle*; 1651: *cofradía* founded; 1652: written *cofradía* statutes; 1670: first modification of statutes	1803: *cofradia* statutes modified; although the Consulado de Bilbao and the Casa de Contraction are located in Bilbao proper, Portugalete continues to function as the 'proper' harbour of Bilbao
Santurtzi	1075: first mention; 1318: existence of old town and church confirmed	1561: activities confirmed without proper harbour facilities; 1690: first mention of existence of *cofradía*	

Sources: Ciriquiain Gaiztarro, M. (1951) *Los Puertos Marítimos del País Vasco*, San Sebastián: Txertoa; Erkoreka, J. I. (1991) *Análysis histórico-institucional de las cofradías de mareantes del País Vasco*, Vitoria: Eusko Ekuntza; Urzainqui, T. and De Olaizola, J. M. (1998) *La Navarra Marítima*, Pamplona: Pamiela Etxea.

Studying the table, we can clearly observe a continuum starting with the official acknowledgement and the granting of special rights (*fueros*) in the twelfth and thirteenth centuries, leading to gradual formalization of the fishermen's confraternities in the fourteenth, fifteenth and partly in the sixteenth centuries. These developments are followed by the further rationalization and improvement of the related infrastructure, a process which continued into the eighteenth century and beyond.

What the table does not make explicit are two slowly developing 'squeezing out' or differentiation processes. The first one relates to the earliest harbours and *cofradías*, which were located at the mouth of rivers providing easy access, but which did not prove viable enough to survive into modern times. The location and environment of the harbours in question did not allow for the newer generation of fishing vessels to dock, and while some fishing continued, they were slowly squeezed out by their neighbour ports. The main examples were Zarautz, Deba, Ea, Mundaka and Plentzia. Their business was taken over by Getaria (Zarautz), Mutriku (Deba), Lekeitio (Ea), Bermeo (Mundaka) and Bilbao and, again, Bermeo (Plentzia). The second differentiation process had to do with two huge joint harbour complexes, that of Pasaia and San Sebastián and that of Bilbao and the other ports situated on the river Nervión. These big harbours developed merchant activities to such an extent that an internal division of labour developed between merchant and fishing activities (with the simultaneous existence of *cofradías* and a consulate as in the case of both San Sebastián and Bilbao). This differentiation was followed by a later and further distinction which had an impact on the entire Cantabrian coast, namely that between two huge and exclusively merchant ports versus all the other smaller fishing harbours. (The case of Bilbao versus Bermeo is a good example.) However, the process did not stop at the rivalry between two ports; it later involved the entire coast in the sense that Pasaia/San Sebastián and Bilbao, together with the Nervión ports, came to dominate the merchant trade while all other ports became harbours where fishing was the dominant form of activity.

So far we have followed the gradual process that led to the founding of the *cofradías* and the gradual improvement and differentiation of the related infrastructure of the Basque ports up to the beginning of the modern era. Towards the end of the eighteenth century signs of change became visible. In particular the new liberal ideas began to question and challenge the medieval structure of the *cofradías* with their exclusivity of representation and their local monopoly of trade. But it was not until the beginning of the nineteenth century that some of these new ideas became sufficiently active to begin to threaten the existence of the *cofradías*. The political and judicial process of implementation proved to be rather complex and often inconsistent.[25] In 1813, for example, a new law was introduced that declared freedom of industry. Just two years later, in 1815, the law was withdrawn – only to be re-introduced in 1820. The validity of the law was finally re-confirmed in 1834 by royal decree.

In relation to the Basque Country in particular, one association subscribed heavily to the liberal agenda, the *Real Sociedad Vascongada de los Amigos del País*. This association, made up of Basque and Spanish intellectuals and enlightened liberals, saw their task as one of liberating rural Basque society from its medieval conditions and pushing it into modernity. As part of that agenda, the society conducted various campaigns against the *cofradías*, which in their mind represented the old regime. The central government took their advice seriously and issued official decrees against the *cofradías* in 1842 and again in 1847. However, the process continued to be uneven and contradictory and in 1848 the existence of *cofradías* was re-confirmed. In 1864 there was a final official attempt to abolish them but this move was again rejected. The *cofradías* survived the legal wrangle mainly because the liberal alternatives and models were not really viable or strong enough to have a significant impact. During the course of the nineteenth century, at least in the Basque Country, no industrial-capitalist fishing project developed that could pose a challenge or even replace the old institution of the *cofradía*.[26]

25 Here and in the following paragraphs I again follow Erkoreka (1991, 73f).

26 The Basque *cofradías* differed from their Cantabrian, Asturian and Galician counterparts further to the west, where the traditional collective decision-making bodies of fishermen were abolished and the fishing sector became subject to industrial development much earlier. (Erkoreka 1991, 80; Astorkiza and Del Valle, 1998, 5ff).

Two other interrelated factors to which I have briefly alluded earlier also helped. The first was the peculiar sense of *hidalguía*[27], which was derived from the old *fueros*. It meant, by contrast with the caste-cum-class system of other parts of Spain, that the Basques all considered themselves to be of noble blood and therefore of equal standing. Whether real or only perceived, a sense of equality was part and parcel of belonging to the fishermen's brotherhood and gave it a meaning beyond mere rhetoric; here their voices were not only heard but the fishermen also experienced solidarity and a sense of togetherness on a daily basis – something that is important to know when one is working in a hostile environment such as the sea. The second factor was that naturally such feelings were encouraged through the fact of being members of an exclusive and monopolistic *gremium*. Against the shared experiences of the brotherhood the new liberal ideas sounded like a threat – not only in terms of putting lives at risk through individualizing the work at sea but also by going against a traditional way of life which had for a very long time provided basic social security and income. In the next subchapter we will take a closer look at how exactly these institutions functioned and also how the *cofradías* tried to find a new balance between tradition and modern requirements in the face of major change and crisis.

3.2 Function and Crisis of the *Cofradía*

In the previous pages the differentiation process and division of labour between the various merchant and fishing ports, the consulates and *cofradías*, have been referred to. In what follows the focus will be exclusively on those ports and *cofradías* which dealt mainly with fishing. I will first examine the functions that the *cofradía* maintained from its origins up to

27 *Hidalguía* derives from *hijodalgo*, son of honour.

the late eighteenth century. Second, I will sketch out the developments from the early nineteenth century up to the present day.

Although the statutes of the different *cofradías* represent the particular local conditions and constituencies from which they derive, they also shared and continued to shape many common features and traditions and were, with very few exceptions, similar in the way they operated.[28] The functioning of the *cofradía* until the late eighteenth century, and how it related to the local community and the local administration or the larger environment such as other ports and *cofradía*, must be imagined as being structured like concentric circles. The inner circle consisted of the local confraternity or the brotherhood itself, including all those who were directly involved in fishing in a particular port: first of all the owner of the boats or vessels, the *maestros* and *dueños*; then the working crews or fishermen the *marineros* or *pescadores*; and finally the helping hands and apprentices, the *grumetes* and *muchachos*. We have to add to this group the people who, elected and employed, worked for the *cofradía* and guaranteed its proper functioning, such as the executive head of the *cofradía*, the *mayordomo*, the chief accountant or auctioneer and his bookkeeper, the *contestador*

28 Representative of all fishermen's brotherhoods is the following modern self-description and definition of the *cordial* of Orio. Its statutes state that 'The Cofradía de Pescadores de San Nicolas de Orio is a co-operative association of fishermen whose objective is to serve the said group, to expand the cultural relations amongst its associates, to provide social security for its associates and to work within the fishing industry without intervention or the help of intermediates … For this purpose its aims are as follows: 1. to organize collectively the sale of the catch of its associates; 2. to lend support to their culture and their professional activities; 3. to establish social security; 4. to organize collectively the export and the conservation of the fish; 5. to facilitate the buying of all effects and articles necessary for professional fishing purposes' (quoted in Garmendia Larrañaga 1979, 151).

Thalamas Labandibar (1935, 112) provides his own minimal definition, in which he describes the *cofradía* as 'a mixed confessional association based on co-operation and mutual help among its professional members whose main objective is the sale of fish.' He adds later that the *cofradía* also functions as a place where interests are mediated and that the regulation of the market is also one of the *cofradía*'s main objectives (113).

and *contra-contestador*, the signalmen, the *señeleros*, and so on. On occasion direct family dependents of members, representatives and employees would also have had access to the *cofradía*; however, they would not have had the right to vote.

In permanent contact and exchange with the *cofradía* we find a wider circle of people consisting of buyers such as small and larger fish merchants, acquirers of fish and tinning factories, intermediate buyers for national and international markets, and so on. Occasionally, one would encounter other workers, people involved in port activities which might be directly dependent on the *cofradía*'s infrastructure such as ship-launching and ship-building facilities or workers from building companies or associations contracted for the maintenance of the port infrastructure. Furthermore, we have to include the local political administration, which, as we will see, often linked up and had numerous contacts with the *cofradía*, although the two always remained separate bodies. Finally, in the outer circle, we might list those contacts that the *cofradía* had with the neighbouring ports and other *cofradías* and, on occasion, with the relevant provincial or state agencies and authorities.

The most important powers in terms of decision-making rested with the general assembly of the confraternity, the *junta de cofrades*.[29] In its annual meetings it elected an executive council which represented the interests of the assembly for the time being. On occasion other meetings could be called; however, they would have no legislative function and were rather of a consultative character. They mainly addressed specific matters which required immediate attention and decisions and which usually could not be dealt with in the annual meeting. They included the conditions for sailing, the determination of local quotas, the discussion of changing prices or the settling of internal conflicts.

29 In the following description of some of the formal aspects I follow mainly Erkoreka's study (1991) and the historical documents that are reprinted therein. However, on occasion I have also included information from other sources such as Thalamas Labandibar (1935), Garmendia Larrañaga (1979), Bikandi (1989) and Gracia Cárcamo (1985).

The initiative in calling for a general assembly lay with the *mayordomo*, the head of the *cofradía*, who was also elected during the annual meeting. However, during election time the mayor of the town was often present, functioning as president and overseeing and ensuring the order of the annual proceedings. To guarantee full representation, the statutes of the *cofradía* demanded that all members helped out and were present at the annual meeting. In the early stages the assembly took place in a church or one of the local hermitages but progressive secularization led to a situation in which the general assembly came to be held in local *plazas*, hospitals, the house of the *mayordomo*, some sheltered place within the harbour or – at a later stage – within the proper facilities of the *cofradía* itself.

The *mayordomo* fulfilled the role of acting head of the assembly. Sometimes two *mayordomos* were elected (effectively 'job-sharing'), whereby the older person usually had the final say. This had the advantage that during temporary absence, such as illness, or in the case of something more serious such as death, the other *mayordomo* could continue with the task of representing and steering the *cofradía*.[30] The job of the *mayordomo* demanded a full-time presence, and because of this commitment the acting head was not allowed to go out to sea or to hold any other job. Since he was in control of all the financial aspects of the *cofradía*, he was also not allowed to bid in the *subasta*, the public auction of the *cofradía*, where the catch was sold and over which proceedings he often had to preside. For his activities and commitment he was reimbursed, either by being guaranteed a fair share of the sale from the overall catch or by receiving a regular salary.

Once elected *mayordomo*, the person could not opt out but had to accept. A re-election was usually not possible.[31] Naturally, the *mayordomo* should be a respected and knowledgeable person with good communication

30 Some *cofradías* had statutes which also provided for a president, often somebody respectable from the community such as the mayor of the town. However, the president's role was only representative. His function was to preside over the annual assembly and to guarantee a peaceful meeting and to lend his authority to the lawful and orderly proceedings, such as the elections of the *mayordomo*.

31 Only later would some *cofradías* allow for it but only when no other person emerged or became available.

skills. In most *cofradías* he had also to be of higher standing, most usually a *maestro* or *dueño* of a boat or vessel. Election procedures allowed for more than one candidate (the number of candidates depending of course on whether one or two *mayordomos* had to be elected). The rules and regulations vis-à-vis the election procedures varied from *cofradía* to *cofradía* and were sometimes not explained or made explicit in the statutes. The normal method was that of exiting through the door of the assembly, sometimes requiring a second round (and exit). There were also variations in terms of the number of votes required for victory. In some cases a simple majority was enough; in other ports it was necessary to have the absolute majority of the votes.

The *mayordomo* could not fulfil all the functions of the office. He was supported by a team, which guaranteed the proper functioning of the *cofradía* and its related infrastructure. Since the administration had to account for its activities and report back to its constituency, it was of utmost importance that the books were kept in proper order. For this purpose most *cofradías* employed a *contador* and a *contra-contador* (the chief accountant and his book-keeper) whose task it was to go through the accounts and to make sure that the books were kept in order. Most *cofradías* retained the office of auctioneer special (the *ventador*) whose role was to preside over the public fish auction. Most *cofradías* also had a limited number of other staff, occasionally referred to as *guardas*, who provided security and functioned as watchmen. Other lesser jobs consisted of helping out whenever necessary, for example keeping an eye on the catch or doing minor jobs during public auctions. An important office was that of *señero* (the signalman; sometimes there was more than one) whose task it was to control the arrival, docking and departure of all boats and vessels. The *señero* also had to make sure that the decisions taken by the *mayordomo* – often in consultation with others when it came to weather conditions and security and to the question of granting permission to sail or not – were enforced. Before the arrival of personal watches and home clocks, it was sometimes also the *señero*'s task to organize the wake-up call for the fishermen. Originally, the *cofradía* also had a person known as *atalayero* (the watchman), whose task it was to spot the whales from the watchtower and to inform the fishermen and whalers that a potential catch was within their reach. Most *cofradías* also had a *capallan* whose task was to stay in close contact with the local church, chapel or priest to organize various religious functions for the fishermen; after all the confraternity had started out as a deeply religious organization.

The most important event that was, and still is, of central concern to every *cofradía* is the public auction and sale of the fish. The basic rule of a cofradía and its very *raison d'être* can be summarized in the maxim that the preferred arrangement would be one where the fish that goes on sale comes from local waters, has been caught by local fishermen and is preferably sold locally to local buyers. Ideally, the whole process takes place in a time frame that allows for maximum freshness, that is, within the shortest possible time between the actual catching of the fish and the sale of it in the *cofradía*. Such ideal situations and their regulation probably referred to a practice in the early development of *cofradías* where communication along the coast was limited, transport complicated and methods of preserving fish very simple (salted and marinated were the only known forms until the arrival of modern refrigeration technology). With time the rules were relaxed and provisions were made which addressed and regulated other more flexible scenarios, such as the possibility of home-based vessels selling their catches in another harbour, non-locally-based ships coming to the harbour and selling their catches, agreements between *cofradías* about respective payments made, and so on. This flexibility was also made possible by improved communication, transport and preservation methods.

Before actually describing the sale and public auction we must ask 'why sell in a controlled and centralized market?' From the point of the *cofradía* the answer would be that it prevents the decentralization of the sale. It avoids a situation where fishermen compete individually for the timing of the sale and it avoids and discourages personal deals. At the same time the collective sale would still reward individual effort and would allow for individual gain. Furthermore, selling in a public auction has the advantage of influencing and regulating prices; most importantly, minimum prices can be introduced. The public auction also provides a scenario where there is enough of a critical mass to establish reasonably large supply and demand sides; finally, it guarantees regular transactions since the day and time of the public auction are made known in advance. The actual sale and its preparation proceed usually in the following fashion: before the sale a demonstration or sample of the fish that is to be auctioned is prepared and made ready for inspection so that the potential customers and buyers know what they are buying.[32] As for the Dutch auction[33] itself, the scenario that Thalamas Labandibar describes for the 1920s still remains unchanged – apart from some minor technological advances – to this day:

> The mayordomo of the cofradía is seated in the lower part of the auction room and the buyers sit higher up on the gallery.[34] The seats that the buyers occupy are numbered and everyone is holding a ball with the number of the seat on it. A pipe connects all the seats with the mayordomo's board. The voice of the mayordomo indicates the price for which the fish is available on the market. Normally the price starts high and then goes down gradually and is always announced with a loud voice. When a price has been reached that is convenient for the buyer, the buyer releases his ball through the pipe, which then reaches the mayordomo at his board. This is followed by the announcement of the buyer confirming the amount or quantity he is willing to buy. (Thalamas Labandibar, 1935, 102f)

32 What is described here in one sentence is actually a very complex process in which experience and insider knowledge are crucial. See also the next footnote about the actual auction and the knowledge that it demands in terms of being a reasonable or good seller and buyer.

33 A 'Dutch' auction is an auction where the auctioneer starts from the top with a high price and calls then successively lower prices, and accepts the first bid. In a Dutch auction there are no bidders at the initial high price. As the price falls at some stage it falls to the level of the highest reservation price, at which stage the relevant bidder makes his interest of buying at that price known to the auctioneer (and then gets the goods at that price). This is in contrast to an 'English' auction where the auctioneer starts off at a low price and calls successively higher prices. At first there may be many bidders, but these drop out until there is only one left. I thank my economist colleague, John Sheehan (University College Dublin), for this information.

34 In Thalamas Labandibar's description it is the *mayordomo* who functions as the auctioneer. In some ports the role of the auctioneer is actually described as that of the *ventador* (seller) or *contador* (accountant). The latter was also often nick-named *cantador*, a play of words: the auctioneer-accountant (*contador*) announces the prices in such a way that it sounds as if he were singing (*cantar* = to sing).

The process described here refers of course only to the organizational *form* in which the sale takes place. Much more information – too complex and varied to be described here in detail – goes into the actual buying and selling process.[35] After the auction and after the catch has been unloaded from the vessel it is then time for the *partija* or *inauta* (the redistribution pro rata), which also includes the contribution to the *cofradía*.[36] The *cofradía* receives its share, the *manta*, from the *monte mayor* that is realized from the sale of each vessel's catch and before all other costs (that is, before the

35 As with dealings that take place in a stock exchange, all kinds of information are necessary to make the appropriate decisions in the shortest period of time. From the seller's viewpoint it is important to reach the harbour at a time when the demand is high and supply short. This arrangement depends on other vessels landing at the same time or on other auctions in nearby harbours. It is useful to know the prices that were paid in the most recent period, depending on the type of fish itself and its quality. The general rule applies that the earlier the fish reaches the market the better. An early entry would allow for later, alternative decisions that would have to be taken in case the calculated price or the minimum price has not been reached at the first auction. A second auction or selling of the fish in another nearby harbour could then still be considered as an option.

On the buyer's side some interests overlap with that of the supplier, yet diverging interests have to be taken into consideration as well. Again, time is a crucial factor. A late landing and auction might help to minimize the opportunity of the supplier to try somewhere else or to achieve a certain price in a second auction – an advantageous pressure point for the buyer. However, a late auction also puts pressure on the buyer; it means he has less time to deliver the fish to its final destination (a market, a restaurant, a fish factory) where freshness is of utmost importance. The question of reliance is also crucial and in the case of fish often calls for compromises: fish does not appear in the same regular quantity as quality agricultural produce; hence, there is even more of an effort on both the buyer's and seller's side to deliver a quality product as regular and timely as possible – and with that comes some form of compromise. Anything short of such a compromise can sometimes have detrimental consequences such as the fish being destroyed rather than sold under value – with the result of the facilitator and fishermen being left unpaid and the buyer empty-handed. Such scenarios are not unheard of but they are rare. The very institution of the *cofradía* was invented to avoid such conflict and to allow for market mediation.

36 There are various models of sharing, pending the type of embarkation. I will come back to these models at a later stage.

reparto or *monte menor* from which the facilitator and crew are paid).[37] The *cofradía*'s share varies from port to port and from period to period but generally does not exceed six percent of the *monte mayor* (Delgado Cendagortagalarza 1998, 48). It should be pointed out here that the payments from the proceedings of the sale do not constitute the only income for the *cofradía*. Additionally, the *cofradía*'s budget is also made up from payments for staying in the harbour, embarking and leaving the harbour and the taxation of 'non-home-based' sales. Furthermore, the *cofradía* can impose and collect fines.

Out of the overall budget, the *cofradía* takes care of the social provision for its members, pays for cultural and religious services and on occasion contributes to the maintenance and development of the related infrastructure. One of the most frequently used provisions is that of social assistance. Whenever members of the brotherhood are prevented from working because of sickness or poor health, accident or bad weather, the *cofradía* intervenes and provides assistance. In the past, the payouts came first in the form of 'naturals', that is as a direct provision from the overall catch. Later the needy received a certain percentage of the sale; in modern times the benefits and payouts have been separated from the actual landings and sales and the needy receive a fixed daily sum.

Cultural and religious services such as funerals (deadly accidents of fishermen occurred then even more frequently than now) are another activity that received regular financial support. The *cofradía*, as an institution with a religious origin, has always supported the local parish, be it in the form of paying for an altar, contributing to the construction of local churches and hermitages or contributing to and celebrating the holy days and fiestas, particularly those related to the three saints of fishermen: San Pedro, San Nicolas and San Telmo. More specifically and directly related to sea-faring activities, the *cofradía* also paid for special masses, for example at the beginning and at the end of expeditions, for embarkations before crews and their ship left the harbour or when a new vessel was being launched

37 Occasionally the contribution is also referred to as the *mareaje de Santa Clara* or the *soldata de San Telmo*, etc.

or for funerals of *cofradía* members. The *cofradía* also organized and paid for a banquet for all its members; the banquet usually coincided with the end of the fishing season or the annual assembly and was often held on the same day that the religious calendar has reserved for the celebration of one of its seafaring saints. The *cofradía* also became increasingly involved in activities aimed at reducing costs for both fishermen and *armadores*. This usually happened through providing tools (hooks) and other equipment such as nets. Very often a supply of bait was also provided by the *cofradía*. Last but not least, it was in the interest of the *cofradía* to maintain and constantly improve its facilities and the related infrastructure, such as offices, auction hall, storing places, workshops and – of prime importance – the piers, launching pads, anchorage, and signals.[38]

One of the most important aspects of the *cofradía* related to the rights and the jurisdiction it held for both the access and the right to fish in a known and well-demarcated area of coastal waters, for the sale of the produce that had been extracted from these waters and for all civil conflict that may arise in relation to that work. This included aspects of anchorage, loading and unloading, all matters of transport to and from the port, sanitation, the sale of fish, the quality of the product, work-related issues

38 From the sixteenth century onwards it was also the task of the *cofradía* to contribute both financially and with manpower to the *levas de marinera*, the levies that kept the Spanish royal fleet afloat. The high economic and social costs seriously hindered the further development of the *cofradías* and had a serious impact on the political economy of fishing on the Basque coast. In a study of Bermeo's contribution and taxation levels Gracia Cárcamo has shown that the levies were so high that they almost bankrupted the local *cofradía* and in one particular year almost stalled all its activities because the levy made up 82 percent of the entire outgoing expenses of the *cofradía* budget. Such high levels have led to a discussion of how far politics determine economics. Furthermore, one might speculate why in the end the Spanish lost the naval race against the British. The high levels of taxation may also explain why there was no capitalist take-off phase or at least some form of primitive accumulation, which could have led to such a take-off (Gracia Cárcamo: 'Las levas de marineria y la cofradía des pescadores de Bermeo en el Siglo XVIII', in: Gracia Cárcamo, J. et al. (1983) 97–134).

such as sailing times, determining the start and end of the season, holidays, mediating between conflicting parties, contractual matters and so on.

It is with respect to such judicial matters that external relations sometimes proved to be problematic. Guarding and taking care of a specific terrain of coastal waters and the local landing place led necessarily to disputes with both the powers that were and boundary disputes with other fishing communities.[39] The issue of boundary maintenance was solved by clearly explaining in the statutes and in agreements between *cofradías* what waters and which harbour infrastructure were under the local *cofradía*'s jurisdiction. These agreements not only defined the boundaries but also all the other legal procedures that would follow from such agreements (definition of 'territorial waters', harbour use and contributions for home-based and extraterritorial vessels, landing fish in ports other than their home port, settling disputes amongst associates and so on). The second issue was more of a legal and sovereignty issue and was not as easy to solve. Most rights had been granted through *fueros*, firstly from Navarre and then reconfirmed and granted by the conquering power, the Crown of Castile. The traditional rights and the related jurisdiction had allowed for a relatively peaceful existence, providing a stable environment and guaranteeing a basic sustenance for the fishermen. As has been pointed out in the previous chapter, these traditional rights came into conflict with the attempt to 'señoríolize' Gipuzkoa and Bizkaia. The Crown of Castile, which had conquered the area, tried to impose its own rule and customs on the newly occupied territory by turning it into *señorios*. Though Castile reconfirmed and continued to grant *fueros*, these *fueros* were no longer part of that multilayered integral legal *fuero* system as had been the case with Navarre, but the politics of granting rights from Castile must rather be understood as a gesture to secure loyalty in a give-and-take policy. The give-side consisted of granting *fueros* to *cofradías* in a highly selective way, often favoring one

39 Furthermore, and this would only apply at a later stage of the development, the very design of the *cofradías* meant that they reserved exclusive rights and were by definition against a competitive agenda that would promote free access for all and question the liberal political agenda of 'every man or enterprise on its own'.

community while restricting and withdrawing support from the neighbouring fishermen's societies. The take-side comprised occupying the local administration in order to gain control of the *señorío*. This give-and-take policy contained many contradictions and could with hindsight almost be interpreted as a cultural-political 'trench warfare', which – depending on the local situation in each community and *cofradía* – would last not only for decades but in some cases well into the nineteenth century.[40]

40 Alberdi Lonbide has described this 'trench war' in more detail in an essay about the situation in the Gipuzkoan harbour town of Mutriku/Motrico, entitled 'La Cofradía de Mareantes de San Pedro en la Historia Pesquera de Motrico' (unpublished and undated manuscript). Lonbide interprets the larger conflict as one that, in microscopic form, took on the shape of a conflict between the local community of fishermen and the local council and its interpretation and application of the *señorío*'s administrative law. Only when the *cofradía* was instituted and became a legal body in the second half of the sixteenth century – again, in itself not a conflict-free process – did it put the fishermen in a better position to defend their rights and economic status. From then onwards the struggle of the Mutriku *cofradía* proved to be so successful that for a few decades the *cofradía* even owned large parts of the harbour. For the complex history of the Mutriku harbour and *cofradía* see also Arrieta 1996, 99–130.

At a later stage the interaction between local councils and *cofradías* seems to have been less conflict-ridden. Erkoreka (1991a, 174–190) for example talks about a positive separation and functioning of different spheres in terms of separating the council's administrative and legal duties from the *cofradía*'s economic and judicial performance. Pursuing common interests became the norm rather than the exception, particularly when it came to the realization of common projects such as improving or modernizing harbour facilities. The conflict between the *cofradías* and the municipal and local government level seemed to have cooled off. Only two cases are really exceptional: The first case is the *cofradía* of Elantxobe, which initiated and organized the split from the rural Bizkaian community of Ibarrangelu, which led to the founding of a new town around the activities of the local fishermen's confraternity. It is the only case in which the *cofradía* directly interfered with the political administration and structure. The second case is that of Lekeitio, where local rules established that the *cofradía* had to be represented on the town council. The cooling off of the earlier conflict could be explained by a change of view: after all, the local elite did not see the *cofradía* as a threat to their immediate and long-term interests; and, secondly, the *cofradía* did not plan a revolution but was, after all, just looking after the interest of the fishermen. Again, this proves that in terms of political history-making

Even though the history of the *cofradías* shows an impressive record as an institution which contributed to the livelihood of thousands of fishermen and managed to do so successfully over centuries, its history was not problem- or crisis-free. In what follows, I will address firstly early crisis points such as the issue of internal representation and redistribution measures. As we will see, these issues caused some conflict; even in relatively small communities there was enough socio-economic space to allow for 'exit' and the creation of a new *cofradía* when some faction's 'voice' was not heard. Solutions other than exit strategies were also pursued; but all in all, these conflicts did not manifest themselves as a universal crisis of the *cofradía* per se. They remained temporary or isolated and limited in character.

The original idea of the *cofradía* was to represent all those in a given community who were exclusively involved in fishing activities, to the benefit of all active participants.[41] In this the *cofradía* was supported by religious ideas, which also promoted the praxis of sharing, appropriate brotherhood behaviour and mediation in case of diverging interests and internal conflicts.[42] However, it would be wrong to see the *cofradías* as institutions

---

and influence the contribution of men who work the waves as fishermen is almost negligible. (This is different in the case of mariners who contribute to the ruling of the waves – a very different, and almost inevitably violent activity.)

41 Erkoreka (1993, 52–55) lists four conditions for access: 1. being a certified believer, i.e. being a member of the church; 2. local residency; 3. 'purity of blood', which sounds rather racist to twenty-first century ears but refers simply to the idea of being part of the *hidalguía*. In other words one had to be a noble Basque. Since all Basques considered themselves to be noble under *fuero* laws, these criteria never had any major impact in the Basque Country itself. (Actually, there is not one historical document or known case where this custom led to any exclusionary practices in fishermen confraternities.) However, the story differs considerably once Basque cofradías begin to operate away from home; for more details see Alfonso de Otazu's magnificient study *El espíritu emprendedor de los vascos* (2008); and (to continue with Erkoreka) 4. payment of a membership or entrance fee.

42 Apart from stating the obvious purposes (religiously founded brotherhood, mutual help) of the *cofradías*, the early *ordenanzas* laid out simple rules and regulations such as respecting specified holy days, the precise contributions to church and crown, the jurisdiction over local waters (including their exact description), what to do in the case of the death of a fisherman, provision for widows, early social insurance such as

where complete equality prevailed. They could not have lasted if that was so. The *ordenanzas* indicate some early level of stratification whereby mariners and *tostartekos* were seen as simple members while the *maestres de pinaza* took all the important decisions (Gracia Cárcamo 1985, 371ff). In some cases the *txos*, the younger apprentices – often the sons of mariners or *maestres* – were not allowed to become members with full voting rights or were not allowed to voice their opinion. Furthermore, conflict regulation had usually more negative consequences for the simple fisherman while the *maestre* remained unpunished. Also, strong controlling elements such as harsh fines in the case of malignant gossip about the *mayordomo* indicate that there must have been some signs of discontent amongst the members of the brotherhood. Yet, although there were clearly signs of disquiet, it is probably fair to say that in the early days of the *cofradías* conflict was somehow limited and contained.

The early practice came increasingly under threat, particularly under conditions where there was a minimal division of labour and where the communitarian efforts were enforced by the need to work as a team under very difficult and sometimes life-threatening circumstances. From the seventeenth century onwards a hierarchical and sometimes even 'aristocratic' element became prevalent (Erkoreka 1991, 124ff and Erkoreka 1993, 49–61). The executive council of the *cofradía*, the *junta*, became dominated by the decisions of the owners of fishing vessels, a process which led first to a metamorphosis in composition and finally resulted in a total monopolistic usurpation through and total hegemony of the *maestres* and *dueños* (Erkoreka 1991, 128). Such new power relations also found their appropriate legal expression in the modified *cofradía* statutes in the nineteenth century, which declared that the position of the *mayordomo* and other leading roles must be held by a *maestro* or *dueño*. The main argument used to legitimize such a prominent position in the assembly was that each owner represented a

---

support for the injured or handicapped and medical support and the obligation to keep account books so that costs for the members were kept to a minimum; some of the representatives' functions such as that of the *mayordomo*, the *contador*, the *señelero* and so on; occasionally agreements with other nearby harbours, or references to joint efforts in *compañías* could be found.

crew and therefore additional representation was seen as unnecessary. Such praxis excluded not only those who should have been represented and who came under such professional labels as *marineros*, *tostartekos*, *tripulantes* and *remeros*, but also excluded those who fulfilled all those tasks without which the whole process would come to a complete standstill, namely that of the *grumetes*, *muchachos*, *txos* and *aprendices*. Furthermore, the new power structure made it possible for the voices of those involved in related activities such as shipbuilding, harbour maintenance work or fish market transactions to be excluded from the decision-making procedures (Erkoreka 1993, 50 and 60f). It seems to be a contradiction that at the moment when the division and differentiation of labour became really important, and more and more people became involved in the process, such exclusionary methods were applied. Particularly from the sixteenth century onwards when increased technology and capacity allowed for sailing and fishing further away and led to longer absences of the men, increased participation of women became noticeable not only in preparing or picking the nets but also in the area of market transactions and commerce. Yet the protocols of the proceedings of the *cofradías*, which would usually record all other voices, remained remarkably blank when it came to such participation (Baroja,1990, 180f; Olaran y Mugica in: Gracia Cárcamo 1983, 18f).

Modernization came very late to the Basque fishing ports and *cofradías*. There were two phases in the modernization process of the nineteenth century, one a prototype and the other a fully developed model. The prototype of industrialization took off slowly, with the number of vessels and fishermen increasing steadily to such an extent that it broke all previous records. This process started in the first half of the nineteenth century and is particularly visible in the developments in the two biggest fishing ports, Bermeo and Ondarroa.

Today Bermeo and Ondarroa are the only Basque fishing ports which have fleets that practice coastal fishing (*pesca de bajura* or *costera*), high sea fishing (*pesca de altura*) and international deep-sea fishing (*pesca de gran altura*). Yet this has not always been the case. In Bermeo the development seems to follow first a 'natural' progressive trend in the sense that it has been a port with a great fishing tradition since the middle ages. It developed naturally in the sense that more and more fishermen and boats took to the sea. The more sophisticated forms of high and deep-sea fishing are a development that only became prominent around the beginning of the twentieth century with the development of the motor and modern techniques of refrigeration. Ondarroa's case is even more illuminating: until the mid-nineteenth century Ondarroa's fishing community did not stand out in terms of numbers. However, once the port facilities had improved (including the canalization of the mouth of the river Artibai), and once the motor and refrigeration had become standard, the industrial fishing fleet increased enormously – to such an extent that Ondarroa became Spain's fourth biggest port and its fishing fleet became one of the biggest in Spain.

What can be observed in both cases is the rapid 'take-off' and rationalization process, which followed once a new infrastructure (better port facilities for larger ships, better transport and communication systems once the fish has been landed) were in place and modern technology (sonar, radar, new cooling systems such as refrigeration) allowed for the introduction and widespread application of new fishing methods such as trawling.[43]

As the cases of Bermeo and Ondarroa demonstrate, the fully developed model of industrialized fishing only came about in the last few decades of the nineteenth century with the arrival of steam engines first and later the diesel motor.[44] Their full impact became only noticeable in the 1920s with

43 For a detailed historical study of the Bermeo and Ondarroa ports and their fleets see Moraza (2000) and Rivera (1997).

44 According to Thalamas Labandibar (1935, 97) the first proper use of a motor on a fishing boat occured in San Sebastián in 1877. Erkoreka (2003, 266ff) lists the following crucial developments: In 1916 there were still only ten motorized fishing vessels in the largest fishing port on the coast (Bermeo); in the 1920s the first trawlers (*barcos del arrastre*) arrived in Bermeo; by the mid-1930s the diesel motor had become widespread; in the 1950s sonar technology arrived; in the 1960s hydraulic mechanisms and in the 1970s radar technology were gradually introduced. Another study of the developments in Orio (Martin Bermejo in: Rubio Ardanaz 2003, 59–93) lists the following technological developments and periodizations: introduction of steam motor vessels: 1915–48; diesel motor and gasoline-based motor: 1947–50; cooling-system and refrigeration: 1947; elevated and towering bridge: 1947–60; sextant: 1951. At a later stage the technology would become even more advanced.

the increased application of the new technologies, in which – as pointed out above – the production of energy allowed not only for faster transport but also for longer storing hours and refrigeration times, thereby making new fishing techniques such as trawling possible.

Until then the fishing communities in the ports and the workings of the *cofradías* had virtually remained unchanged. In the mid-1920s there were between 6,000 and 7,000 fishermen working on a coastline that was about 60 miles long; 1,600 were based in Bermeo and about 1,025 in Ondarroa alone.[45] The fishermen were exclusively organized in 18 *cofradías* located in 16 ports,[46] seven of them in Gipuzkoa and nine in Bizkaia (Labandibar 1928, 103 and Eusko Ikaskuntza 1925, 320).

The fishermen's income consisted not of a regular paycheck at the end of each week or month but resulted from the sale at the public auction in the *cofradía* and the redistribution according to the type of embarkation and expedition.[47] The model of sharing was not only dependent on the type of

---

According to the Orio-study, sonar was introduced in 1955, hydraulic systems in 1965, radar in 1974, the plotter in 1990 and heat detection systems in 1995. Although these observations apply only to the developments in Bermeo and Orio, they seem to be fairly representative of what was happening in other Basque ports at the time.

45 Both Thalamas Labandibar and later Martin Bermejo point out repeatedly that for each fisherman one has to calculate a family of five or six members to get an idea of how important the income from fishing was to the families and the towns which depended on fishing.

46 At the time of publication of the protocols of the Asamblea de Pesca (1925), the Gipuzkoan port of Orio and the Bizkaian port of Ondarroa had two *cofradías* each. The two *cofradías* that existed in Bermeo had just been re-united and the two Ondarroa *cofradías* were about to link up again (in 1926). The split into two *cofradías* in at least three ports with ongoing discussions in other ports hinted at some serious disagreement about the direction the *cofradías* should take (both in terms of internal representation and fishing regulations).

47 The data available for Bermeo in the case of bonito and tuna fishing are as follows (based on a crew of twelve and one *patrón*): 50 percent for the *armador* (facilitator) and 50 percent for the crew. The crew's 50 percent was then divided up between *patrón*/captain 3.45 percent, 6.84 percent for food and the engineer, and 1.72 percent for cleaning and netting; the rest was then divided up between crew members. For anchovy campaigns the following model applies: 66.67 percent for the *armador*, 27.15

expedition but also, increasingly, on whether the embarkation was based on rowing, sailing or a motor, with the result that the advantage lay with the *armador* when it came to the new type of motor-based vessels.[48]

With the new technologies work patterns became more differentiated and would eventually lead to disagreement and conflict. Compared to prior crisis points and conflicts, this time the crisis was real and could not

---

percent for the crew, 2.46 percent for the *patrón* and 1.24 percent for the *chicas*. In the case of besugo the numbers are as follows: 52.78 percent for the *armador*, 40.73 percent for the crew, 4.63 percent for the *patron* and 1.86 percent for the *chicas* (Thalamas Labandibar 1928, 104). When studying the numbers one has to take into account that absentee ownership is not a practice widely followed along the Basque coast. Usually the *armador* is also the *patron* (the normal model) or works as a fishermen (this happens rarely but occurs occasionally). Depending on the situation, one has to read the above numbers accordingly.

Thalamas Labandibar does not explain whether these models are based on the share from the *monte menor*. I assume it is from the *monte menor* because it does not refer to the payments to the *cofradía* and the so-called dog's money, which usually came from the *monte mayor*. The dog's share – in Basque: *txakurrena* – refers to the fact that many vessels had a dog that was used for smelling the fish that came close to the surface and sometimes jump in mid-air and thereby helped the fishermen to spot the fish in the open sea. On return to the harbour the dog was usually rewarded and given some share of the fish (one) – the so-called dog's share. Since all crewmembers had the right to some personal reward this amount became known as the dog's share (Bikandi 1989, in: *Itsasoa*, 156).

48 For rowing embarkations the numbers are as follows: 54.45 percent for the *armador*, 44.44 percent for the crew and 1.11 percent for the *chicas*. This differs clearly from the sailing model in which 26.22 percent goes to the *armador*, 65.57 percent to the crew, 6.56 percent is held back for reserves and 1.65 percent goes to the *chicas*. For the older type of motor vessels the numbers are 57.15 percent for the *armador* and 42.85 percent for the rest (Thalamas Labandibar 1928, 103f). Clearly a case can be made that this model does not reflect in any ways a new source of income for the *armador* but just the increasing costs for the new type of embarkation based on motors. However, as we will see later the new technology also allowed for an increased division of labour – traditionally consisting of capital in the role of facilitator/*armador*, technical knowledge in the role of captain/*patron* and labour/crew – to which were now added the engineer, the greasers and soon other specific types of labourers. It is worthwhile noting that the engineer was the exception; he received a salary because his work continued even when the ship was docked.

be contained or solved by just referring to local conditions and traditions. Particularly the introduction of new fishing methods such as trawling (*pesca de arrastre*) and the lack of appropriate *cofradía* regulations for the catch stemming from such new fishing methods, together with the increasing power of the buyers, such as fish factories and wholesale fish merchants, led to major debates.[49]

In 1925, under the auspices of the newly founded Basque Studies Institute, Eusko Ikaskuntza, representatives from all ports came together to discuss the new situation. The *asamblea de pesca* called for major reform (Eusko Ikaskuntza 1925, 320ff). Against the oligarchy that had come to dominate the *cofradías* but also against the threat of massive exit from the *tostartekos* who were no longer content to be dominated by the *maestros*, *dueños* or *armadores*, and who increasingly opted for creating or joining alternative *cofradías* (as they had done in Bermeo where the *tostartekos* had left the *armador*-moderation and compromise). The forum conceded that over time a division between labour, technology and capital had evolved which could no longer be controlled by either labour or capital. However, the assembly also suggested that exiting and founding competing *cofradías* in the same port was not the solution. A sector that might be dominant in a given community on the coast was not so powerful when compared to the overall economic performance of the provinces, hence it was necessary to stay together and to represent the fishing communities with one voice.

In an attempt to overcome the crisis, the Assembly made some concrete suggestions to improve labour and capital relations and to modernize the general workings of the *cofradía* (Eusko Ikaskuntza 1925, 332ff). As to labour–capital relations, the Assembly suggested as a model the Elantxobe statutes, which allowed for representation according to the size of each embarkation, thereby allowing the non-owners to have a major voice in the *cofradía*.[50] The Assembly also called for the integration and

49 Very often the conflict was not just limited to a conflict between individual communities but very often within communities as the history of the *cofradías* in Bermeo and Ondarroa clearly demonstrates.

50 This suggestion fell clearly short in terms of turning the *cofradías* into fully functioning co-operatives. However, many of the ideas that were floated in the Assembly

institutional inclusion of women without whom the *cofradía* could not function.[51] They also suggested that a proper fund (*caja*) be instituted at the *cofradía* to provide for the case of crisis or long absences from fishing (*días de casa* or *etxe egunek*). This fund would replace the medieval system of occasional individual payouts, which had become unworkable because of the increase in the size of most *cofradías'* operations and the large numbers of fishermen involved.

As to the modernizing program the Assembly made a number of further points. They included suggestions to strengthen the professional character of the *cofradía*, to simplify its administration (for example by instituting a *caja de ahorros*, which separated and simplified financial payouts), to expand into full-flung co-operatives with full modern merchandising capacities, including industrialized fish-production and appropriate sale

---

resembled co-operative ideas that were the currency of the day. In the Basque Country the cooperative movement has always been very strong (Olabarri 1985, 299ff). Its origins were many-sided: they could be either *patronal* i.e. initiated and funded by a rich and benevolent capitalist, or have their roots in either socialist workers' initiatives, social Catholic groups, purely co-operative movements or sometimes have an inter-class aspect. Its origins lie somewhere between 1848 and 1906, which was the first take-off period, followed by a second period from 1906 to 1914/17 when first laws considering co-operatives were introduced and the first common funds, *cajas*, established. A third phase from 1914/17 to 1931 followed. It witnessed the first co-operative congress in Barcelona with the participation of various political groups (UGT, CNT and UCNE). The period from 1931 to 1936 witnessed an exceptional development in terms of co-operative movements, which clearly blossomed under the republic. The big names that are associated with the Basque cooperative movement are Toribio Echevarria (Alfa group), Polycarpo Larrañaga and Alberto Onaindia (ELA/STV, mainly Catholic) and Jose Marie de Arizmendarrieta (Mondragon co-operatives).

Although the *cofradías* did not become full-flung co-operatives, this did not prevent individual vessels and embarkations from taking on the form of co-operatives, a form that is not unknown in Basque ports, although it remained the preferred form of a clear minority of fishermen.

51 Here, the Assembly's recommendation does not refer to the general gendered division of labour in fishing communities; it relates rather to such harbour-related activities as netting, buying and selling and other market activities.

facilities, and to centralize and form a federation, a *Unión de Cofradías* with central offices so that negotiations and co-operation with the Fishing Ministry were made easier. (This last point was particularly important if the *cofradías* wanted to develop and handle proper *pósitos*, i.e. execute bank or insurance-like functions like other cooperatives.) The proposal to modernize also included important gestures towards the past. It was seen as important that the *cofradías* retained their confessional dimension and that their cultural traditions and contributions should in any case be preserved.

Not everything developed as the Assembly had envisioned. A report from 1936, commissioned and published by the Madrid-based *Sociedad para el progreso social*, attempted at a comprehensive analysis of the situation of the fishing industry in the Basque Country (Gandasegui Larrauri 1936). At the time of writing there were seventeen *cofradías* out of which fifteen were now legally also *pósitos de pescadores* (seventeen *cofradías* altogether, if the two *cofradías* of Bermeo that remained split are included). They organized 3,939 associates in Bizkaia and 1,751 associates in Gipuzkoa – all together 5,690 individuals. The study also referred to a minority of fishermen who were not associated, 71 in Bizkaia and 160 in Gipuzkoa.[52] Instead of showing unity in the way they functioned, the report referred to a differentiated situation where now three different types of *cofradías* and statutes co-existed: those which limited the participation to *armadores* and *patrones* only, those which admitted only *tostartekos* (where the *armador* and *patrón* were also included but received no special acknowledgement or elevated status) and those which had representations of both *armadores* and crew (Gandasegui Larrauri 1936, 22f). The administrative functioning of the *cofradía* was still the same but now properly structured with a representative board, the *junta directiva*, including a president, a

52 The report also gave a breakdown per port. For the Bizkaian ports the numbers for *cofradía* members are as follows: Bermeo: 860 (exterior port) and 850 (interior port); Ondarroa: 1,100; Lekeitio: 480; Santurtzi: 207; Ciervana: 196; Elantxobe: 116; Arminza: 87; and Mundaka: 43. For Gipuzkoan ports the numbers are: San Sebastián: 440; Hondarribia: 336; Mutriku: 312; Getaria: 282; Zumaia: 140; Orio 80; Pasaia de San Sebastián: 84; and Pasaia de San Pedro: 77.

vice-president, a secretary and a speaker, administrative staff including the *mayordomo*, an administrator, a first, second or third accountant, and the technical personnel consisting of signalmen, lighthouse men and guards. The practical function of the *cofradía* had now two clearly specified dimensions: firstly, the *cofradías* had to regulate all aspects of labour relations amongst the members, the decision about docking and landing, the modes of entry and exit to the local port and the determination of the terms of all contracts including – most importantly – the sale of fish.[53] Secondly, the *cofradías* now provided social security in a more comprehensive way by administering the common funds, the *pósitos de pescadores*, particularly in the case of emergency, injury, incapacity and enforced periods of lay-offs; additionally the *cofradía-cum-pósito* arrangement provided help in terms

53 As before, all *cofradías* followed the 'Dutch' public auction system whereby the auction starts at the top of the price-range and is then counted down. The model was based on the experience of auctions along the coast and guaranteed what seemed – at least on the surface – to benefit both sides, supply (the fishermen) and demand (the buyers, by now mainly fish factories and larger fish merchants). However, over time an auction that starts top-down discourages the bidders ever to go for the highest price at all; it makes a sale much more likely to concentrate at the lower end of the scale, particularly when there are big buyers who are in contact with each other and share some information about prices; and it fails when expectations from almost-daily auctions have established stable prices independent of how and under which conditions the fish was caught. For more details see Rivera Medina (1997, 101f).

Both Gandasegui Larrauri (1936, 28) and Delgado Cendagortagalarza (1998, 52) mention a short experiment in the Bizkaian port of Santurtzi where the auction started, the 'English' way, i.e. 'bottom-up'. The experiment lasted only fifteen days and the bottom-up model then changed again to the top-down model. Retrospectively, the Santurtzi experiment must be seen as a last ditch attempt of the supply side – the fishermen – to make their voice heard and change the system. Yet market conditions and power relations had changed beyond recognition. The demand side, the big fish factories and wholesalers, now influenced the market to such an extent that they could determine the conditions of the sale – hence also their boycott of the Santurtzi experiment. We must assume the enormous pressure, helplessness and disappointment of the supplier in this case: after all, a strike or boycott of fishermen makes little sense – a strike or boycott against whom? There are only so many times one can dump the entire catch into the harbour.

of medical insurance, pharmaceutical help and payouts in the case of death or work-related accidents. There was a noted absence in terms of cultural and religious activities; we can assume that by this time the *cofradías* were no longer exclusively religiously defined brotherhoods but had become a mixed institution partly fulfilling state functions.[54]

There are few long-term studies that show the development in the fishing sector and its problems in a nutshell. However, one such study is available: Delgado Cendagortagalarza's community study of Bermeo describes the developments that took place in the largest fishing port on the Basque coast between 1912 and 1955 (Delgado Cendagortagalarza 1998). His study pays special attention to the conflict over fishing methods which took place in the local *cofradía*. The most important expeditions that were conducted from Bermeo in the time period concerned were so-called *kosteras*, (sometimes also referred to as coastal fishing, *pesca de bajura* or *pesca litoral*) catching *bonito* (white tuna), anchovies, sardines, *besugo* (sea bream) and *merluza* (hake).[55] Yet while the modern *bajura* expeditions introduced somewhat newer fishing methods such as using live bait (*cebo vivo*), a method which only became possible with the solution of the energy and conservation problems, those expeditions still differed considerably from trawling.

54 As any current observer will be able to testify, Basque fishermen of course continued to remain deeply religious people and until this day attend religious services. The difference is that they do this now no longer in a group-led fashion or inspired by an institution (the cofradía) but rather on an individual basis. Very few other cultural activities, such as banquettes or fiestas, are now cofradía initiatives, although this can occasionally still happen.

55 Bermeo became the biggest fishing port on the Basque coast. In 1935 it accounted for 101 vessels alone (in contrast, the second biggest port, Ondarroa, only had about half of that, 48 vessels). If one calculates for each embarkation a crew of twelve men, this brings the number of fishermen up to more than 1200. In 1955, Bermeo's fishing sector had risen even beyond that number and accounted now for more than 2000 fishermen (Delgado Cendagortagalarza 1998, 45). To be sure, not all of these were involved in *kostera* expeditions, particularly since the *pesca de altura* was also pursued from Bermeo (together with Ondarroa and Pasaia). In any case, the majority of Bermeo fishermen were certainly involved in *kostera* expeditions.

As Delgado Cendagortagalarza points out (1998, 48), *kosteras* and *bajura* expeditions operate subject to certain constraints, such as the cycles of economic activity which in turn depend on seasons and seasonal activity (no fish, no economic activity); they further depend on the industrial production of the tinning industry, which by then had begun to determine the demand side and therefore impacted heavily on the price. These circumstances have led to a very insecure situation for the *armadores*, *tostartekos*, *txos*, and the small independent fish market buyers (usually the wives of the fishermen). With the exception of the engineer, part of whose salary is fixed since he works both on land and at sea, the others involved do not receive a regular income or salary but depend entirely on the sale from the landed catch and the circumstances and conditions under which it was brought to the market.[56]

The price that was actually achieved in the sale would add to these basic insecurities. The market price that was paid could – as has already been pointed out earlier – depend on many factors but certainly the fishing methods applied mattered a great deal. In the case of Bermeo a period of unregulated fishing methods between 1901 and 1908, in which trawlers were allowed to fish in coastal waters (that is, within the six-mile zone), impacted so heavily on the catch of the *costeras* that it led not only to a dangerous situation where the nets that were used in trawling almost destroyed the coastal fishing stock and grounds entirely but also had consequences for the *costera* expeditions and those people who worked on the supply side of an already fragile market. New regulations concerned with trawling did not solve the problem: trawling outside but near the six-mile zone still had the effect of continuing to deplete the coastal stock. At the same

56 The basic model of redistribution still had not changed much. According to Delgado Cendagortagalarza (1998, 48f) the model looks as follows: from the *monte mayor*, 6 percent go to the *cofradía*; furthermore, the common costs for crew and facilitator are deducted; from the rest, the *monte menor* or *reparto*, 50 percent go to the *armador* and 50 percent to the crew. From the crew's share the *patron* receives 3.45 percent, 6.84 percent are deducted for food and 1.72 percent go to the women involved. The rest is equally divided between crew members with the only exception being that a *txo* gets half of what a full crew member would get.

time and of equally important consequence, the interests of fish factories and wholesale buyers did not take into account how the fish was caught as long as it reached their factories in time and in the quantity that was needed. The demand side – by now 70–80 percent of all catch landed went to fish factories – began to determine the market completely. Even the introduction of minimum prices, which must be regarded as a worthwhile attempt by the supply side to regain some control of the market, did not stop this process.[57]

What prevented the process from getting completely out of hand was the property structure of the supply side. Co-ownership and small mixed forms of ownerships of vessels (up to five people) remained the norm and big capital investment and absentee-ownership the exception. What also helped was the actions and decisions that the fishermen took themselves to voice their opinion and to represent their interests appropriately. Bermeo's *cofradía* had a long history since its founding in 1353 and it had in its past, like all the other *cofradías*, dealt with various minor conflicts and crises. It also reflected the general tendency of these institutions in that from the seventeenth century onwards an oligarchic process could be observed in which the decision-making powers lay mainly with an aristocracy that was formed by the owner of vessels, the *armadores* and *dueños* (Delgado Cendagortagalarza 1998, 60f). The differentiation was finally formalized in the new statutes in 1886, which stated that in order to become a member of the executive junta one had to be either facilitator (*armador*) or a captain (*patrón*) of a vessel. By the turn of the century such monopolization of power through the owners was no longer seen as democratic and inclusive. In 1907 tensions between political factions became manifest and a split occurred over the question of whether the fishermen's interests were fully represented vis-à-vis the interests of the *dueños*, *maestres* and *armadores*. A considerable number of liberal brothers from the Cofradía de San Pedro felt that their voice was not heard and that the *tostarteko*'s contribution

57 In the case of Ondarroa, Italian *salazoneros* and merchants completely dominated the market, especially the anchovy market, in the first four decades of the twentieth century. For more details see Moraza (2000, 156ff and 211ff).

to the overall functioning of the *cofradía* was not fully taken into account by the nationalist-Catholic faction. They decided for the exit option and founded the Cofradía Goizeko Izarra. Another split occurred in 1913 when the Catholic dynasty came into conflict with the radical nationalists. The nationalists instigated reforms, although their demands were less radical than that of the liberals who had left. The nationalists tried to convince the remaining Catholic faction to respect the traditional balance between capital, labour and technical staff and urged them to avoid class conflict. Their practical reform model suggested that the crew should be given a vote to represent their interests (Delgado 1998, 62f). To be sure, this was an improved offer and better than no reform at all, but it certainly fell short of the liberals' original democratic demand of one man, one vote. Furthermore, the suggestion of turning the *cofradía*'s funds into more comprehensive *positos* – a policy that the Second Republic encouraged the *cofradías* to implement in order to provide for improved social security – was not pursued any further. But even this more moderate package was not acceptable to some. The result was another exit, this time from the Catholic faction, who founded the Cofradía Santa Clara.

Eventually the liberals of the Cofradía Goizeko Izarra were reconciled with the former San Pedro brothers and rejoined the old confraternity in 1924. The saga did not end there. In 1932 the Cofradía de San Pedro split again, this time into a Cofradía Interior and Cofradía Exterior, a split that would last until the year Franco came to power. Whatever the internal political splits were, what remained of the *cofradías*' genuine and common contribution was the regulation of at least some important aspects of coastal fishing; thus, they reached some conclusions vis-à-vis trawling and the preservation of the coastal fish stock which were far more long-sighted than anything that had been suggested on the demand and buyer's side. What the *cofradías* could not change or even stop was the increased power and still-growing influence of the demand side. Looking back, the conflicts and splits between Bermeo's *cofradías* demonstrate the limitations of a perspective that sees fishermen as a class and the debates within *cofradías* as corresponding to class relations. Such a perspective usually undervalues the social relations that are formed on board which resemble family or father-son relations more than capital-class oppositions. In other words, it is hard if not impossible to detect something like a class conflict on board. Furthermore, the *bajura* fishermen have never been a salaried class dependent on the capitalist entrepreneur; they only receive an income from the actual sale of the catch and the bottom line that applies is that when there are no fish, there is no income. But most importantly, the bigger powers that influence to a certain extent the sale (and thereby the income) are clearly outside the *cofradías*' – and therefore the fishermen's or the *patrón*'s – competences and power.[58] The *cofradía* and its functions are indeed limited in terms of what can be achieved with respect to influencing those market forces which increasingly have taken control and determine to a large extent the general conditions of the sale.

As the history of the conflict in and among the Bermeo *cofradías* suggests, the big split is not between *maestres* and *tostartekos*. Their relationship is not conflict-free, yet it appears to be minor when compared to the split between the supply side of fishermen and the demand-side of big fish manufacturers and merchants.[59] Trawling is one aspect of this relationship; it threatens the *cofradías* and fishermen's existence and works to the clear

58 In Ondarroa this meant a change in the very conditions under which the sale took place. However, since the *cofradía* still organized the sale there remained still some built-in advantages for the seller (the fishermen).

59 The class conflict therefore takes place in the form of positions in market relations. In a study that Sesmero has conducted (Sesmero 1997, 221ff) about intercommunity relations in Bermeo the results show that the social stratification, which is a result of the conflict between *cofradía* and fishermen on one side and fish-manufacturing on the other side, also found its architectural expression: while the fishermen live close to the waterfront and the port, the commercial class lives in the better flats and apartments up-town. The irony of this situation cannot be lost: the fish-manufacturing class indeed lives and works free from the conditions of the sea.

Sesmero also notes that when it comes to housing, there are finer distinctions within the *arrantzale* group, particularly between those fishermen who have made it into the vessel-owner group and those who remain simple *tostartekos*. However, these are fine distinctions and do not contrast as much with those who belong either to the supply or the demand side of Bermeo's unique form of class struggle.

benefit of the demand side. This unequal relationship is the key to understanding modern fishing and the way *cofradías* work in modern times.[60]

60 It is important to note that the Basque *bajura* fleet has not given in or become resigned to the powerful trawler and fish industry and has, until this day, kept up with technological innovation and developments. Particularly the method of fishing with live bait has helped the fleet to stay afloat; it has refined the technique of *artesenal* fishing and is a unique example of sensible rationalization that does not throw all older experiences and insights over board – a genuine example of reluctant modernization. For more information about this kind of moderate rationalization and innovation see Bikandi's study 'Aspectos sociales de la actividad pesquera. Ciclos laborales y compañías' (Bikandi 1989, 149–174).

Bikandi looks particularly at the changing aspects and roles of both *dueño* and *tostarteko*. While in the past the *dueño* was first and foremost a representative of an entire family and head of a proper *casa*, the situation is now very different. The clan may still be part of the family background but has become less important as the *patrón*'s knowledge is no longer handed down from one generation to the next and has made space for the new role of the knowledgeable *patrón* and proprietor who through his experience contributes considerably to the crew's income (149). Especially when it comes to new methods such as fishing in a *compañía*, the crew will rely on the contacts and knowledge shared between various patrons. A *compañía*, consisting of a maximum of five or six vessels (usually from one harbour although not exclusively so) can be formed either prior to leaving the harbour or spontaneously when reaching the fishing grounds. The *compañía* works in such a way that all caught fish is loaded onto one boat which will return to the harbour to sell the catch while the others continue fishing. The way the money is shared differs from the usual procedure. The redistribution model for a *compañía* that consists, for example, of three vessels would look like this: three vessels agree beforehand or spontaneously form a *compañía*; they 'plough' the same territory; the catch from the three vessels is loaded onto one ship; this ship returns to the harbour and from the sale the common expenses or debts of the formed *compañía* are paid before each vessel gets its one-third of the share. The idea of *compañías* is that of fewer overall expenditures; less time is wasted in the harbour and more energy is saved. However, the formation of *compañías* depends on the informal knowledge of and trust amongst the *patrones* that form part of the *compañía*.

Another way of minimizing risk and organizing 'luck' is of course in continuously upgrading the technology of the vessels. This again demands a changed role from the *patrón* and owner. It is no longer enough to have accumulated all historical knowledge and to be a good captain. The very high costs that are involved in running a modern

At the beginning of the twenty-first century, it seems a miracle that institutions that originated in the twelfth century still keep functioning – although, as we will see, in radically changed fashion.[61] As the story told so far suggests, the *cofradías* had to adjust to a constantly changing environment. In the past, conflict and crises had occurred repeatedly but did not become explosive issues in the sense that they questioned the very *raison d'être* of the *cofradía*. This situation only lasted until the first decade of the twentieth century. Today the *cofradías* face a very different situation. What has changed is, first, that it is now difficult for the *cofradías* to determine or influence the agenda in a radical way. In other words, what has changed is

---

vessel also demand from the *patrón* excellent communication skills and experience in reading the fishing situation. No crew will catch fish when the bridge is manned and managed incompetently. (This, by the way, could in the past sometimes lead to situations where the most experienced man stands on the bridge and that he might or might not have been the *patrón* of the boat; today it is almost certainly and with very few exceptions the *patrón*.) For the type of knowledge that is required to steer a modern fishing vessel see the informative study by Martin Bermejo in: Rubio-Ardanaz, J. (2003), 59–93.

61 At the beginning of the new millenium the Basque fishing fleet consists of 468 vessels with 4,236 crew, 2215 of them in the *pesca de bajura*, 979 in the *pesca de altura* and only 220 in the trawling industry (*arrastre*). The rest consists of ships that specialize in catching either cod (251) or tuna (571). The number of people working in the entire fishing sector is approximately 27,000 (Gobierno Vasco, in: Rubio-Ardanaz, ed. 2003, 60). For the entire Basque Autonomous Community this does not sound like much. However, for the coastal towns and ports that depend to a large extent on fishing it is a considerable number of people that are employed in the sector and, apart from the economic importance, fishing also represents a way of life. It is even more regrettable, then, that the recent offers of retirement for entire parts of the Basque fleet, mainly due to a problematic fishing policy of the European Community, has left some Basque ports with nothing more than just a symbolic representation of what was once a thriving fleet. This is particularly noticeable in smaller towns like Mutriku or Lekeitio, which were once thriving ports but which now only host small-scale and mainly private activities (mostly for pensioners) – not even enough to keep their respective *cofradías* open for most of the day. However, while some harbours and *cofradías* show little port and fishing activity, other ports and *cofradías* – like Getaria for example – seem not only to thrive but also seem to have capitalized from the decline of some of the smaller harbours.

that the power of initiative now no longer lies with the supply side (i.e. the fishermen) but with the big fish-marketing industries. Second, and this is the point to which I will turn now, today most of the professional fishing is subject to a complex web of legislation and governmental interference – a situation which impacts particularly on the different types of surface fishing methods (Apraiz and Astui 1989).[62]

Within the new rules one has to distinguish between local, regional, national and international agreements and laws (Apraiz 1987, 188ff). While the local laws and customs are still a matter for the local *cofradías* – they determine the fishing seasons and inspect the types of hooks and nets that are being used – the regional federation of cofradías of Gipuzkoa and Bizkaia regulates and oversees the various zones; they also determine whether certain types of fish can be caught in a given zone or whether a prohibition applies. It is at the national level that the regulation of trawling is decided; and as we have seen, extensive trawling has been one of the biggest environmental threats to the *cofradía* and coastal fishing in the past. The main issues concerning trawling seemed to have been solved in 1953 when a law was passed that prohibited trawling in waters below 125 metres deep. In 1962 those regulations were revised; trawling was allowed within the six-mile zone but not in waters below 100 metres in depth. In 1965 the rules were tightened; they now also prohibited trawling within a six-mile zone. In 1969 this zone was extended to twelve miles. On an international level the most important regulations concerning coastal fishing consist of bilateral agreements between France and Spain but increasingly

62 To be sure, there is some flexibility in the way these terms are being used (Apraiz and Astui 1984, 119). The *pesca costera* is limited to 15 tons and the average embarkation has a crew of three to four. The type of fishing (red snapper, monkfish, sea-rock fish in general) is with hooks and *artesenal*, that is, not industrial but based on individual effort, commitment and capability. The *pesca litoral* is up to 60 tons with an average crew of six to seven. The main catch is hake, bream and bonito and usually lines and hooks are the preferred tools. The *pesca de bajura* is in vessels up to 200 tons with a crew between fifteen to twenty fishermen. The catch consists usually of anchovies, bonito, tuna, sardines and mackerel. The fish is caught with middle-sized nets and with rods and hooks.

the European Union has a say in this as well, particularly when it comes to determining quotas. For example, the Spanish–French agreement from 1967 states that it is prohibited to fish in each other's waters within a three-mile zone off the coast; limited 'foreign' fishing is allowed within three to six miles, while in the six to twelve mile zone both sides are permitted to fish. Increasingly other factors have become important; under the newly established EU quota system it is now possible to fish in 'foreign waters' if one holds a licence.

Basque fishermen are also very active in the *pesca de bajura* which extends beyond coastal fishing and reaches as far as Asturias, the Azores, the African coast and even South America and the Indian Ocean. (Apraiz and Astui 1984, 74ff). The type of fishing is mainly with middle-sized nets and rods and hooks. Until the nineteenth century there were hardly any rules regulating this type of fishing, and since it was done with hooks, middle-sized nets and lines it did not seem to be as problematic as trawling – mainly because of its limited amount, which was determined by the methods mentioned. Furthermore, the buyers were middle-sized companies, which did not exercise the pressures that the national and multinational fish industries exercise today. In particular, the *cofradías* still exercised some influence when it came to self-imposed regulations. In 1883 the first national regulations ruled about the use and size of nets, and from 1906 onwards catching dolphins was prohibited. In 1974 the first regulations for catching *bonito* with live bait (anchovies) were introduced. In 1980 FROM (Fondo de Regulación y Organización del Mercado) was founded, the first state organization that attempted to regulate the export and import of fish. In 1987 a new federation of *cofradías* was introduced, establishing minimum prices and regulating the beginning and end of campaigns; the new federation also introduced maximum quotas for each embarkation.

The *cofradías* managed to survive into the twenty-first century but not without changing their role and function considerably. In the past the *cofradía* had been concerned with regulating everything. Today, it has a much-reduced competence while other bodies (such as the federation) have become more important. Its tasks and powers are still considerable; they include the sale of fish (though in a much reduced format since the fish factories and wholesalers avoid the public auctions and usually buy directly from the big fishing companies) and the supervision of prices for the fish that are still sold at public auction. The *cofradía* can also still enforce the rules and is also still, literally speaking, the 'first port of call' in the case of emergencies and rescue operations. As we reach a new level of national (state) and international agreements and intervention (European Union and international fishing quotas), and while catching methods are being constantly revolutionized – today fishing with the help of ships that look rather like floating fish factories and even including helicopters is common – the traditional role that the Basque *cofradía* once played seems to belong to the past. Yet, it would be too early to suggest that the *cofradía* as an institution is about to die or fade away entirely. As new issues such as sustainable fishing, ecological matters and healthy nutrition become important, the *cofradías* could potentially become part of the solution.

In a recent study of fishery policies and the potential new role that the remaining *cofradías* can play, its authors suggest a major re-orientation and re-consideration when it comes to modern *cofradía*-related policies (Astorkiza and Del Valle 1998). It is worthwhile at this point to use Astorkiza and Del Valle's contribution briefly in order to reflect briefly on the history and the changing functions of the fishermen's *cofradías*, from their consolidation in the fifteenth and sixteenth centuries, and the almost total power of what was almost a guild-like organization, to becoming an obstacle to the idea of free enterprise in the course of the nineteenth century (6ff). In their overview the authors point out that the Basque *cofradías* managed to maintain their status for so long mainly because of their belonging to the foral territory, which was exempted from the new Spanish civil code legislation when it took effect in 1864. Some limitations were introduced and some changes took place in 1873 when the *cofradías* were forced into complying with free enterprise. Radical changes only occurred at the start of the twentieth century when the *cofradías* adopted new rules in order to comply with the gradual invasion of state-related structures and function. During the Franco regime the *cofradías* became vertical trade unions within public corporations, something that did not cause major protest, mainly because the new policies did not cause a problem for the still prevalent inter-class philosophy of the fishing communities.[63] After the death of Franco newly defined rights and duties became part of the corporate and administrative role of the *cofradía*. Workers and employees were now free to join unions outside the *cofradía*. However, the new laws also meant that the *cofradía* lost its monopoly of representation. In 1978 a royal decree confirmed that the *cofradías* now had the status of a public corporation (just as under Franco) and had, in collaboration with the government, also a consultative and administrative role to play. A further decree issued in 1983 led to a de facto handing over of the authority to the Basque Autonomous Community. The functions remained basically the same: the *cofradías* now had to serve as consultatory bodies, to represent and defend the joined social interests of the fishing community and to provide services and administrative support. The new status under the Basque Autonomous Community created some room for manoeuvre. Particularly insofar as fishing in territorial waters was concerned, the *cofradía* was now again in a position where it could define the areas (of course, only those within its boundaries), the fishing periods, and the means with which to catch the fish. While the new arrangement gave the Basque authorities some control, it seems too little too late. The new European agreements and regulations leave little space for interpretation. Despite its politically correct eco-rhetoric, the European Union has – just like its individual member states – shown very little interest in maintaining sustainable fisheries and local fishing communities.

Summarizing the big changes and developments over the years, it becomes clear that the Basque *cofradías* have, until the early 1980s, always adopted and coped well with the demands of each new historical

63 I do not think Astorkiza's and Del Valle's comment is intended to be offensive. The comment relates rather to what appears to be some structurally conservative social aspects of Basque fishing communities. By no means is it the intention to say that Basque fishermen were sympathizers or anywhere close to the political project of Franco and his regime. The opposite is actually true: one just has to look at the enormous efforts of fishermen to save their fellow citizens from inside encircled Bilbao during the Civil War and the many fishermen who either went into exile or enjoyed the freedom of the sea in some form of 'internal exile'.

constellation. As Astorkiza and Del Valle rightly point out, over time the *cofradía* has come to accept the increasing role of the state in its very functioning. The biggest impact of that development has been that what has once been a historic right has now become a concession. The dilemma is an obvious one: while the *cofradías* might well be able to enforce Autonomous Community and EU regulations, particularly when it comes to the *bajura* fleet, the negative aspect is that the trawler industry has become dissociated from *cofradía* control. While the surface fleet follows self-imposed guidelines, the trawler fleet and its adjunct, the big, internationally-operating corporate fishing industry, show very little self-discipline and mercy when it comes to environmental concerns (13ff). Astorkiza and Del Valle have a point: 'voice' may indeed have finally found a temporary home in the current *cofradía* arrangements, but whether it will be heard or even prevail under such complex international and multi-dimensional conditions as those mentioned earlier is far from certain.[64] Furthermore, cultural and social encounters, which were originally at the very heart of the *cofradía* idea, seem to be in steep decline. As one astute observer has pointed out (Homobono 1989 and 1997) the modern *cofradía* is – regrettably – no longer at the centre of social and cultural activities. It may even be argued that such a relatively new institution like the cooking society or *txoko* or the local fiestas and rituals, which originally took their impulse from the men who were organized in the *cofradía*, may well outlive the older institution that helped to create them in the first place.

64 One of the most moving portraits of the decline of traditional *cofradía* activities can be found in the social-anthropological 'thick description' (Geertz) of Rubio-Ardanaz. (Rubio-Ardanaz, 1994). The story of the displacement of the *mujer sardinera* in the port of Santurtzi describes an irreplaceable loss of a moral economy.

Another more recent example is the legitimate ecological and economic concern that the Basque *cofradías* voiced about the disappearance of anchovies at the start of the anchovy season in late spring of 2005. (This is after having repeatedly warned the Spanish government in the past about declining fish stocks.) While the Basque fishermen and the *cofradías* themselves demanded a complete fishing moratorium, they were first lectured by the Spanish government about representation and later by French fishermen (some of them French Basque) that this would not stop them going out to sea to fish the remaining (and probably last) stocks.

3.3 Reluctant Modernization II: The *Cofradía* as an Attempt to Facilitate 'Voice'

The sea demands a very different organizational form of social and economic life when compared to that of the rural world. Out at sea the crew of a boat or ship works separately from their families, town and community, forming for the time being, but often also beyond the time at sea, strong bonds with their seafaring companions. While the men are working the waves, the women remain on land preparing for and dealing with almost everything that has to do with the landing (picking nets), buying, selling and further distribution of fish and/or the preparation for the next fishing trip (such as flicking and repairing nets). It is the woman who runs the household and takes care of the children. In contrast, the rural and soil-based *baserria* and its occupants rely much more on a joint effort that is less physically separated (although, as we have seen, some differentiation of labour also prevails in the rural world). The differences between the rural and the seafaring world are mainly explicable by their respective unique physical environments that in each case demands different social communication skills and leads to different economic activities. The traditional *cofradía* and its moral economy could only develop and function properly because it was also an expression of a mainly urban or semi-urban environment and culture out of which a plebian culture would eventually emerge. Coastal communities founded in the early Middle Ages were founded with a purpose in mind. The ports functioned not only as communication posts between the coast and the interior but also as communication posts along the coast, directed mainly towards the sea and the people who made a living from it. As distinct from Mediterranean harbours, settlements on the Cantabrian coastline did develop less 'organically'; they were planned settlements and establishments and, as pointed out above, very much of an urban or semi-urban character or type. This distinguished feature can only partly be explained by geographical conditions such as the steep coastline.[65] The dense settlements – not only in terms of distance between communities but also inside each individual community[66] – allowed for a concentrated effort; it created a critical mass and functioning infrastructure devoted to specific social-economic aims. Fishing, trade and emerging small-scale industries (iron, ship-building) were the main economic activities. Fishermen, artisan labourers such as carpenters, hook-makers, *cofradía* employees and small-scale trades people were its main players, and, together with their families, they formed the biggest part of the working population. Other powerful players in the town did emerge or were always present such as the Church or local administrators and other town officials. One feature stands out however, and that is that at no point can we encounter the development of an identifiable elite or stratum that occupied and maintained powerful positions over a long period.[67] If one studies historical accounts of Basque coastal communities of the last five hundred years, it is – apart from the odd *jauntxo* family and villa – impossible to identify something like a local ruling class that reproduces itself constantly and over long periods of time. What one can encounter though are the said three key institutional players, who are all in one way or another an expression of or connected to the plebeian majority of the local community: the *cofradía*, the mayor's office or town hall and administration and the local church. It was this

65 The fact of planned establishments does not contradict the fact that since time immemorial there had been fishing activities along the coast and that these human activities grew as the human settlements and their needs expanded. However, the organized founding of most Basque coastal towns by royal charter from the thirteenth century onwards was to my mind a new qualitative step.

66 It is normal in Basque fishing communities to encounter three- or four-storey houses. Having said that, single family-owned houses do exist but in each community they are limited to half a dozen, maybe a dozen houses. They are often *jaunak* houses (belonging to rich noble families) and are rarely occupied throughout the entire year.

67 In contrast, until the present day if one asks for the genealogy of families one can encounter the pride of belonging to or stemming from a family that has since time immemorial belonged to the fishing or fishing-related sector.

institutional constellation and its supporting social network that allowed a plebeian culture and a stable moral economy to emerge.[68]

It would be wrong to think of this plebeian culture as one of complete equality of conditions, and this is not what the term refers to. What the term signifies in our context is, first, that there is a working majority in the town and that this population mainly depends on seafaring and fishing and related activities and industries; second, that this population knows also some internal distinctions and a certain division of labour to remain functional; third, that it is a working population in which one can hardly encounter extremes, be it in the form of either a significant and powerful super-rich stratum or a segment or layer of entirely deprived people; and fourth, that a stable institutional infrastructure exists to support the working majority in their economic efforts and social and cultural lives. These four circumstances or conditions helped and contributed to the development of a local civic, should we say 'plebeian', spirit and a related culture and economy, something that is unique and that one cannot really encounter in such a highly developed form in other traditional fishing communities in Europe.

As pointed out above, in order to function properly and to have a lasting effect, the solidarity aspects that have developed must take on an institutionalized form and must be adequate to the unique environment. Thus, while the rural environment demands particularly strong relationships with the next-door neighbour, especially in time of need (harvest) and emergencies (births, deaths, essential repairs), being out on sea and working the waves is much more hazardous than work on the farmstead and demands a different common effort. Out at sea there are always conditions that cannot be fully controlled and against which one is not fully protected. There are real risks that one might never return and the great number of fishermen's lives lost at sea speaks of the risks involved. It is therefore not surprising that fishing communities have, from the early Middle Ages onwards, done

68 The most obvious example is the youngest harbour town and settlement, Elantxobe (Bizkaia), where the *cofradía*, a new town administration and the local church, and of course the fishing community, all worked together to establish the new town.

everything to protect fishermen and to organize mutual help, firstly by forming strong bonds amongst the crew and, secondly, by institutionalizing solidarity in the form of the *cofradía*. Once in place, such institutional forms of solidarity have evolved slowly but steadily over centuries and have over time become more and more sophisticated in the way they operate. As we have seen in the previous pages, the institution began as a Christian brotherhood and mutual-help society and was in most cases founded around the same time when official status was given to the respective local town or harbour. In the beginning the *cofradía* was an association without any great infrastructure or built environment. It evolved eventually into a guild-like institution with its own proper facilities, gaining considerable power and control in the local village or town, and amounting to what could be described as a local monopoly-like corporation. What mainly symbolized the beneficial activities of the *cofradía* was the sale and marketing of fish. In order to appreciate fully the functioning of what was new about the market and what made it work it is again useful to refer briefly to how the historian E. P. Thompson has described market and related social activities before the arrival of the modern capitalist relations.

In his essay on moral economy and the English crowd, E. P. Thompson notes that the old economy, that is the economy before capitalism's victory, still knew certain moral rules and regulations (Thompson 1980, 80ff). Developed at subsistence levels of production, the produce and the products of the farm (or from the sea)[69] were usually exchanged directly and without mediation; only later did local or regional markets come into play. But even when markets began to develop everybody still knew one another; the chain of trade was the shortest way possible between producer and buyer and involved few if any intermediaries. If one purchased from Farmer X (or Fishwife Y), one knew usually the quality of the product one was purchasing and the price was usually seen as just or fair in the sense that the buyer thought that the product was worth the amount paid.

69 Thompson always uses the example of the countryside's small towns and markets. Rarely does he mention coastal communities and their exchange mechanisms, something that I am trying to rectify here.

Additionally, production and consumption in the same town or village was based on direct interaction and with that developed trustworthiness. The market place was a space where not only goods were directly traded or sold, but it became a unique experience in its own right in the sense that the crowd which frequented this public space could also experience a sense of its own power, as can be demonstrated by studying the early days of protest against new conditions such as rising bread prices. Because of its direct communication and interactive patterns, there was also a sense of still being interested in and being aware of each other's circumstances and condition (128).

Thompson's description applies mainly to the rural small town and its market, but one just has to add a few genuine features from fishing communities and his description could easily be applied to any *cofradía*'s fish auction. The main features would hardly change: the prevalence of face-to-face interaction and personal trustworthiness, regarding the market not only as an economic exchange mechanism but also as a place where other forms of social interaction can take place, such as trading news, chatting, the common and sociable consumption of food and drink, etc. Even the mention of near subsistence production in Thompson's description would apply to the early fish market. One of the most striking features would be that the market itself is run without middlemen. If we had to find an overall characterization of the activities taking place we would have to say that economic activities were a crucial feature but that these were always still imbedded in other forms of social interaction.

Although the *cofradía* as an institution was founded to benefit all members and their family relations we must not imagine it as an idyllic place where everything is just working to perfection. There has never been complete equality amongst associates in the brotherhood. Between owners (*maestres*), captains and the working crews there were always differences in terms of opinion and interests that also found their expression institutionally, particularly when it came to distributing the share or when it came to occupying the most powerful positions in the *cofradía*. While those differences were real, there was no rule or invisible glass ceiling that would in principle prevent individual fishermen from becoming either small owners or shareholders and from occupying one of the more attractive positions in the *cofradía*. For a very long time, until the arrival of industrialization to be precise, fishermen could always make their voice and concerns heard, either individually or collectively and such sense of 'having a voice' would also naturally extend to economic activities such as the market and the fish auction. No reality matches better Albert O. Hirschman's formula that it is a sense of loyalty (and one could add in this context, solidarity and common experience fostered under the often extreme conditions of the sea) that allows for 'voice' to be heard and keeping protest and 'exit' at bay.

Only with the emergence and differentiation of different types of modern fishing such as industrial trawling and large fish-processing industries did the internal cohesion and solidary aspects of the crews and the *cofradía* erode. Mainly because of the change in labour practices and the sheer scale of the new fishing expeditions, the *cofradía* could no longer hold on to the old forms of solidarity. A split became manifest: on one side the workers and their rather mechanical work patterns – trawling is considerably less artisan than traditional fishing – and on the other side capital, either in the form of an absent ship-owner or in the form of a corporation. Since trawling relies less on individual or collective experience but heavily on technical infrastructure and knowledge that is concentrated in one person (the captain or the owner), it is unlikely that solidarity bonds emerge between captain/*maestro* and crew as they did before the arrival of trawling and industrial labour relations. The crew on a trawler can be hired at any harbour and is usually treated like a group of industrial employees, i.e. their labour power is regarded as a mere commodity. The men are less likely to stem from the same town or village or even from the same family. These circumstances make communication more like that of a factory or shop floor than that between mates or family relations.

The industrialization of working practices on sea and on land, the increased division of labour, and new market conditions changed the fishing sector and the decision-making processes of the *cofradías* totally. Tinning factories, processing plants, better transport, new forms of refrigeration, and the internationalization of the fish market, also brought in outside players;[70] and while new investments helped the fishing sector to expand, industrialization and the involvement of outside capital also meant new class differentiation not just in terms of the split between captain and crew but also in terms of responsible and responsive ownership. In the past, for centuries, there had been small and middle-sized companies, usually family-run, that together with the fishing crews and their dependents determined the policies and politics of the local *cofradía*. This changed considerably at the turn of the twentieth century when the monopoly for landing and selling fish that the fishing fraternities held onto was abolished, mainly due to the demands of a new free market which was influenced heavily by the new incoming capital and its interests.

The old monopoly rights and traditional forms of solidarity did not go quietly. There was indeed a widespread reluctance to modernize, industrialize and capitalize fishing. As we have seen in the cases of Bermeo and Ondarroa – for a long time the two largest fishing communities on the Basque coast – conflict over the issue who had the right to speak and decide ('voice') had been a major feature, and fervent disagreements over the types of fishing, the right to land the fish and the right to market the sale (or to be exempted from it) led to faction-building and finally even organizational splits. Both, Bermeo and Ondarroa, had developed a significant trawling sector and eventually the disagreements over the type of fishing, the timing and length of the fishing seasons, landing and selling rights, etc., led to the founding of new *cofradías*. It meant the end of traditional forms of loyalty and solidarity and the idea that the *cofradía* represented all fishermen and all interests.

Ever since the split emerged, there had been attempts to stay together and re-unite the different interests again under the roof of one *cofradía*. Yet, the industrialization process and the demand of market liberalization that went with it appeared to be unstoppable and made this difficult. In the 1920s nationalist attempts under the aegis of Eusko Ikaskuntza attempted to appeal to all the factions and interests, trying to argue for more unity

70 See for example the investment of Italian companies in Ondarroa and other harbours.

and a more coherent approach towards the controlled exploitation of the sea – but only with limited success and only for a short few years until the beginning of the Civil War. Under Franco the monopoly was somehow artificially prolonged, mainly for political motives and reasons. Francoist fishing policies tried to secure support and misused the *cofradía* as a corporatist institution in which the members had no political and social control. While the monopoly of the *cofradía* was thus artificially kept alive, the economic changes kept eroding the very institution – a process which continued after Franco's death.[71]

At the present time, not much is left of loyalty, the 'voice' of fishermen (collectively or individually) and the old egalitarian ethos of the old-type *cofradía*. The uncontrolled freedom and exploitation of the sea together with the centralization of decision-making processes – first in the form of the local provincial government, later in that of the Basque and Spanish governments, then followed by the European Union – eventually led to a situation where the seas were seen as a limitless resource base to be exploited as if there were no tomorrow. In the end this had disastrous consequences. After years of 'open seas' talk and free market ideology there is now a new awareness and a more protective rhetoric that speaks of ecological balance and sustainability, limited quotas and stricter control. Yet, while ecological rhetoric has now become the talk of the day, the very institutions that could have guaranteed such policies are in an almost moribund state.[72]

71 In an informative anthropological account of and reflection of maritime fishing on the Basque coast, Juan Antonio Rubio-Ardanaz (2006, 30f) has described the long twentieth-century struggle between *pesca artesenal* and *artes menores* (traditional fishing which is economically less profitable) and *pesca capitalista* and *artes mayores* (capitalist and economically more profitable fishing). Rubio-Ardanaz referred mainly to the port of Santurtzi, at the mouth of the river Nervión (now part of greater Bilbao), but his description could, with minor variations, also be easily applied to the harbours of Bermeo, Ondarroa and Pasaia.

72 It can only be called tragic that only a symbolic and sentimental presence of fishing and *cofradía* activities can be encountered in most harbours. In Mutriku for example one can now see two *cofradías*. While the old Cofradía Zaharra has been turned into a museum, the modern *cofradía*, which is now also defunct, offers its facilities to a seafood-processing company and a scuba diving school. The former fishing harbour,

To be sure, there cannot be any going back in time, not at least because the entire socio-economic environment of the old harbour towns has changed. While nowadays one can still detect a sense of old civic 'plebeian' pride and a presence of a rich tradition in the small Basque towns and harbours, symbolic gestures can hardly be substitutes for the plebian spirit and a related moral economy that now belong firmly to the past. In that past the plebeian culture and moral economy dimension could develop because of the existence of common identities stemming or derived from similar or identical working environments such as seafaring, fishing and related activities. Today this is no longer the case. Today only a minority works in the fishing sector and maintains a symbolic presence. Furthermore, harbour towns in the Basque Country have, demographically speaking, developed dramatically over the last few decades. A process that started at the end of the nineteenth century has led to what seems to be an almost unstoppable urbanization process in an area that had already witnessed a considerable density in terms of urban settlement and development.[73] Nowhere has this process become more visible than in the decline and moribund state of the *cofradías*, which once had lent voice to the fishermen but which are now, with few exceptions, defunct. One *cofradía* (that of Mutriku, Gipuzkoa) has already been turned into a museum where the grandsons and granddaughters of former fishermen now can see how their grandparents lived and worked.

---

one of the oldest along the Cantabrian coast, is about to be turned into a sports and leisure harbour. Noisy speedboats and elegant yachts, mainly from France, visit the port now during the summer. During the winter port activities are down to zero. Similar observations can be made in Lekeitio and Zumaia.

73 The writer Bernardo Atxaga has repeatedly stressed that one can regard at least the southern part of the Basque Country as one huge urban environment. It is not by chance that the Basque word *hiri*, denoting city or urban space, is morphologically not that far away *herri*, country or people.

CHAPTER 4

'The Social Bonds of Cooking': Gastronomic Societies and Moral Economy

The origins of the gastronomic society (in Spanish, *sociedad gastronómica*; in Basque, *txoko* a diminutive of *zoco* which means 'corner') lie in San Sebastián, a mid-sized city, tucked away in a *bahía* on the Cantabrian coastline, only a few miles away from the Spanish–French border. Thanks to its central location it developed in the nineteenth century into an administrative centre and became the capital of the Basque province of Gipuzkoa. Due to its prime location and improved communications – trains, electricity, the telegraph and later the telephone had all arrived in a short period of time – the city had over the course of the nineteenth century witnessed an influx of visitors and soon developed early signs of a flourishing tourist industry. This process was accompanied by a change in the composition of San Sebastián's working population. The rural migration from the countryside into town continued throughout the nineteenth and early twentieth centuries and by the late nineteenth century the migrants had already become an integral part of the city's working population.

4.1 Origins, Historical Development and Geographical Distribution of the *Txoko*

The particular history that follows – the rise of the popular societies and especially the development of the gastronomic society – must be understood as the result of an accelerated modernization process, in which both the 'plebeian' element of its working population and the early signs of the tourist trade helped to turn San Sebastián from a mid-sized seaside town into a modern city of cosmopolitan and leisurely character (Aguirre Franco 1983 and Luengo 2001).

Towards the middle of the nineteenth century the city's administration had already recorded the existence of a few dozen establishments in which sociability featured prominently. Some were cafés and appealed more to the entertainment of an upper-class clientele, with billiard facilities and larger tables where *tertulias* could be held; the rest were mainly taverns or *sidrerias*, places where one could have a drink – usually cider – with friends (Luengo 2001, 45). This situation was not going to last and particularly in the city centre the café increasingly came to replace the tavern. The cafés lost their elite and aristocratic character and the urban space that used to be exclusively owned by a few became now subject to a 'massification process' (Luengo 2001, 47)[1] The first popular society *La Fraternal* was founded in 1843 and its foundation can be regarded as symbolizing that change. Its main purpose was to bring together its members for the sole purpose of *comer y cantar*, eating and singing. Soon other societies – mainly of artisan background – would follow.

San Sebastián's main chronicler, Felix Luengo, has pointed towards the social change that had occurred and that would soon express itself also in cultural terms: artisans had begun to dominate San Sebastián's working population; and it was this sector which would soon also become the main protagonist in terms of organizing popular activities and events such as the *tamborrada* (50). Earlier, in the nineteenth century, San Sebastián class and occupational divisions had expressed themselves in vertical and horizontal spatial segregation: the aristocratic elite occupied the high buildings in

1 Luengo notes that it is hard to draw a clear demarcation between the various establishments; however, by pointing to the history of two particular establishments, the *Sociedad Filarmónica* (founded in 1840) and the *Reunión de Amigos* (founded just a few years later and well established by 1850), he also stresses that even at this early stage distinctions were already visible. The former had been founded to entertain the bourgeois sector, while the latter with its café-type design, its reading space, billiard facilities and general liberal ambience was also bourgeois yet less elitist in its appeal (Luengo 2001, 48f).

the centre and partly the old town, while rich seasonal visitors and tourists owned the chalets along the beach at the curve of the *bahía* (57ff). In contrast, the not-so-well-off lived in much smaller buildings in the exterior surroundings and further away from the centre. However, by the second decade of the twentieth century a changing class structure had led to a new arrangement of urban space. Artisans and fishermen, both constituting now the 'plebeian' majority of the working population, had moved into the old town, close to the harbour facilities.[2] As mentioned above, San Sebastián had, from the second half of the nineteenth century onwards, also developed a significant tourist industry. Now, the development went beyond a few rich chalets and found its expression increasingly in tourist-related infrastructure such as the construction of casinos like the *Gran Casino Kursaal* (opened in 1887). San Sebastián witnessed a true hotel and café boom. Big hotels such as the *Hotel de Londres*, *Hotel de Francia* and the *Hotel Continental* all opened for business in the 1880s and more than a dozen new cafés had opened their doors.

Both developments, that of the tourism industry and the changing class structure, led to the further differentiation of popular space. By 1868 the city council recorded the existence of 58 popular establishments, and the number grew to 106 in 1882. Most of these establishments were *tabernas* and *sidrerias* (*sagardotegis* in Basque) mainly located in the old part of the town, which by now was firmly in the hands of artisans and fishermen. However, one of the problems of the taverns and cider places was their early closing hours; by law they had to close at 10.30 at night. A temporary solution consisted of turning taverns and cider houses into cafés, which would allow them to stay open until one o'clock in the morning. A better,

2 Luengo provides the following statistics for San Sebastián's class structure: in 1911 artisans made up 28.27 percent, new working class 18.95 percent, employees and administration 10.32 percent, proprietors, industrialists and free professions 7.01 percent and fishermen, rural employees, clerics and military 19.43 percent (Luengo 2001). The unique constellation in which the 'classic' industrial working class is underrepresented but various subaltern classes together form something like a working plebs, justifies the use of the Thompsonian term 'plebeian' class structure. For a detailed discussion of such class relations see Thompson (1980 and 1991).

long-term solution was to have one's own new mixed-purpose establishment that combined aspects of the tavern, the café, and eating places. For this purpose one had to invent another organizational form – the *sociedad popular* (popular society). An early forunner was *La Fraternal*, founded in 1843, but soon others would follow. The last three decades of the nineteenth century witnessed a number of newly founded societies: *Pescadores de San Sebastián* (1869), *Unión Artesana* (1870), *La Armonía* (1872), *Neptuno* (1878), *Primero de Abril* (1879), *Unión Obrera* (1880), *La Humanitaria* (1892) and *Euskalduna* (1893). The membership ranged from 50 to 80 members. The recruitment showed a clear social profile in that all popular society members were artisans or fishermen and all new foundations intended to be democratically inclusive in terms of membership.[3]

The new societies provided an infrastructure where one could drink, eat, sing and rehearse and prepare cultural events such as plays, parades and festivities like the *tamborrada*. Usually the society would also have a library and a reading room.[4] Another social function of the societies was to integrate migrants not only from the rural environment of San Sebastián but also from other parts of Spain. Later, entire societies would be founded in which the name of the society hinted at the region of origin of its members.[5]

3 Both Luengo (2001) and Franco (1983) stress that the popular societies were usually restrictive only in terms of the overall size of membership but that any discrimination in terms of class was unheard of. The exclusionary practices in terms of sex, which prevailed in the early history of the popular societies but which became less restrictive over time, will be dealt in the discussion of the general function of the *sociedades*. However, it should be mentioned here that *Unión Artesana*, one of the oldest societies remains until today exclusively and explicitly male.

4 A famous incident that has been well recorded happened a few years later. Pio Baroja, the famous Basque writer, had once been invited to *Gaztelupe* one of the best-known *sociedades* but had found the experience wanting after he had been shown the 'library' – the name that members had given to the society's *bodega*.

5 Rafael Aguirre Franco notes the arrival of so-called *casa regionales*: *Centro Burgalés* and the *Circulo Riojano* (1916), the *Casa de Galicia* (1931) and, later, the opening of a Catalan house (1955). It should also be noted here that the rise of the popular societies did not remain unchallenged. San Sebastián's bourgeoisie soon responded

At the beginning of the twentieth century new political movements and parties emerged and changed the political landscape of the Basque Country. In the first instance these were political–organizational responses to the rapid modernization process. In the Basque Country they found their distinctive expression along two major markers, class and national identity. In San Sebastián the different identities expressed themselves also culturally and in different ways; socialists, nationalists, anarchists, republicans but also various unions and social Catholic groups, all established their own societies, thereby contributing to an increased 'democratization of recreation' (Luengo 2001, 102 and Aguirre Franco, 21). Sports of all sorts were an expression of such democratization. Football, mountaineering, cars and car racing, the famous Basque ball game *pelota* and Atlantic rowing *regatas* were no longer restricted to the few but became spectator sports for mass audiences.

The activities described above led to a further democratization and popularization of the culinary *sociedades*. In most cases, this involved an increasing number of women. Nearly all of the newly founded societies responded to the changing constituencies, and to the needs and demands of those participating in the increasingly broad spectrum of new leisure activities. In contrast to the membership of the older societies, which had been dominated by artisans and fishermen, the new societies which developed in the first two decades of the twentieth century, were symbolic of the rise of the middle class in San Sebastián, as they appealed mainly to the new small and middle bourgeoisie.[6]

---

by founding their own private clubs and societies, mainly along the *ensanche*. Most prominently and lasting until the present day were *Maria Christina* (1925) and *Monte Igueldo* (1912). As Felix Luengo has pointed out, these clubs also participated in the organization of the *carnaval* and the *Semana Grande*; however, the *tamborrada* remained exclusively a task of the popular societies (Luengo 2001, 84).

6 Among the new societies listed *Gaztelupe* is, according to Rafael Aguirre Franco, the society of all societies. Not only did it develop the art of singing – *Gaztelubide*, the society's singing outlet entertains like no other formation – *Gaztelupe* is supposed also to have the best wine cellar (Aguirre Franco 1983, 20).

Between 1925 and 1936 San Sebastián witnessed a further major boom; fifty-five new societies addressing and dealing with a wide range of activities such as musical interests, sport, religious activities and culture were founded. The most interesting aspect, however, was a new differentiation process, particularly the development of so-called gastronomic societies, that is, societies whose main purpose was for members to cook and to eat. Certainly, a few societies only devoted to cooking had already been founded at the beginning of the twentieth century, most prominently *Cañoyetan* (1900) and *Euskal Billera* (1901). They were now joined by societies which originally were more interested in sports but had now decided to become cooking societies: *Gimnastica de Ulia* (1917), *Sociedad de Caza y Pesca* (1919) and *Ur-Kirolak* (1922). In the 1920s, new cooking societies developed which had their origins first in republican and then nationalist circles: *Aizepe* (1921), *Gure Txokoa* (1925), *Sociedad Illumpe* and *Donosti Berri* (both 1927) and *C.D. Vasconia* and *Zubi Gain* (both 1928). The coming of the republic was greeted by another wave of new establishments: *Istingarra*, *Itzalpe*, *Aitzaki*, *Gizarta*, *Ardatza*, (all founded in 1932) and *Lagun Artea* (1934). However, the Spanish Civil War and Franco's new regime slowed things down; until 1945 not one new society was opened. The post-war development and new openings of popular and cooking societies appealed more to aesthetic form and design than to widespread usage (Aguirre Franco 1983, 23). But whatever their future course and further differentiation, today it is an acknowledged fact that San Sebastián's cooking societies had not only had a remarkably successful history but have indeed become the city's distinctive modern trademark. There are currently 120 cooking societies in San Sebastián and it is estimated that one out of every 3.5 adults is a member of a *sociedad* (Van Wijck 2000). The popular society in general and the cooking society in particular truly became the intersection points of San Sebastián's civic culture. As an organizational form, the popular society encompasses many activities. It has even become a model for export to other areas, having great appeal in the rest of the Gipuzkoan province.[7]

The history of popular and gastronomic societies is somewhat different in Bilbao and its environs. Resulting from the long history of trade and commerce with England and the enormous affluence of Bilbao, popular establishments in this city first aspired to the ideal of the English gentleman's club.[8]

Clearly the difference between Bilbao and San Sebastián was one of both real and perceived wealth and class distinctions. As an illustration a reference to the history of Bilbao's first popular society is useful: members of the so-called *Kurdin-Club*, which had been established in 1899, tried to imitate the colonial lifestyle of the British (Aguirre Franco 1983, 61ff, Alonso Cespedes 1996 and Egin Monografias, 2f). Not only did they introduce sofas, boot-stools and marble tables to the society but the drinks were also different: cocktails and whiskies replaced cider and wine. That the whole enterprise was meant to be somewhat self-ironic and humorous becomes clear when looking at the rituals of the members of the *Kurdin-Club*: one had to wear caftans and imitate religious practices; additionally, one worshipped certain 'holinesses' such as Martell, Hennessy and Jimenez Lammothe. The irony went even further and clubs within the club were formed: the 'Club de Hatchis', 'Club del Opio' or 'Club del Kiff'. As the first rules of the club state: 'everyone does what he likes' and the motto seems to have been that one has to alienate oneself in order not to be alienated.

It would be wrong, however, to assume from this example that class or wealth alone determined membership. While it is true that the first wave of popular societies in Bilbao was more marked in terms of class distinctions, the further development and history of the *sociedades gastronómicas*

7 Historically speaking the phenomenon first spread to other Gipuzkoan towns, particularly those that were just a short ride away from San Sebastián. The 1920s and early 1930s saw the opening of cooking societies in Tolosa (*Gure Kaiola*, 1927 and *Gure Txokoa*, 1931), in Zumarraga (*Beloqui*, 1929) and in Zarautz (*Gure Kabiya*, 1931).

8 That the English represented an ideal becomes clear when one looks at the history of the city's soccer club Athletic Bilbao – not 'Atletico Bilbao'.

in the city and its environs still demonstrates that equal status within the society still remained the rule rather than the exception, and that even the choosing of a particular society to join by a prospective member was not completely determined by class background.[9] However, the difference between Bilbao and San Sebastián consists of a certain 'elevator effect'. In Bilbao class distinctions have always been more pronounced than in San Sebastián, which never had a history of heavy industrial development, and the obvious and visible stratified social layers that usually come with it.[10]

The history of popular societies, and in particular cooking societies, in Bizkaia begins outside its capital. Their origins can be traced back to Bizkaian seaside towns and ports such as Ondarroa, Lekeitio and Bermeo, following San Sebastián's lead and spreading along the Cantabrian coastline towards the west (Alonso Cespedes 1996, 28). Lekeitio, a small seaside resort, has seventeen societies, while Bermeo, a slightly larger town than Lekeitio, has more than thirty.[11] The oldest purely gastronomic society in Bilbao, with 85 founding members, *Gure Txoko*, was only founded in 1954. It was soon followed by a second society, *Txoko Bilboko Umore Ona*.[12] In the second half of the 1960s and early 1970s a true boom followed, most

9 As we will see later, gender is a different issue altogether.

10 The history of the Basque labour movement, Basque socialism and the Basque bourgeoisie and capitalist class clearly has its origins in Bilbao and its environs – not in San Sebastián. For a history of class and class struggle in the Basque Country see Beltza 1976 and Nuñez 1977. For a detailed study of the history of Bilbao's business elite see Blas 1997.

11 As reported in the Basque newspaper *Deia* (1981). In his ethnographic work on Bermeo, Homobono dates the first *txoko* back to the mid-1960s. Since then there has been an astonishing development; the 1970s proved to be particularly successful in terms of expansion. In Bermeo alone 36 txokos have been founded. Today Bermeo has the second highest number of *txokos* in Bizkaia (after Bilbao). Homobono points out that by 1985 there were some 1,700 members, which is 37 percent of Bermeo's male adult population. Most of them, 75 percent, came from the fishing sector (Homobono 1987, 350).

12 Which one of the two really came first is not so clear. Alonso Cespedes (1996, 31) points out that the *Txoko Bilboko* really came first since it started in 1948 but only registered officially in 1961.

prominent amongst *Achuritarra* (founded 1965) with 200 members, *Sociedad Recreativa Deusto* (1967) with 150 members and *Abando* (1970) with 100 members. At present Bilbao has forty-five societies in total, normally with between thirty to sixty members each (Alonso Cespedes 1996, 121).[13] As in San Sebastián, most cooking societies can be found in the *Casco Viejo*, and in the neighbourhoods of Uribarri and Santutxu; otherwise *txokos* in Bilbao seem to be equally distributed around the city. This can again be seen as a confirmation that despite the existence of a Bilbao business elite, and despite its unique social clubs, popular urban space and related activities are hardly dominated by these.

Just as in Bizkaia, Alava and its capital, Vitoria, took their lead and inspiration from San Sebastián and Gipuzkoa (Idroquilis 1994). But in contrast to Bizkaia, cooking societies developed in Vitoria as early as the 1930s: *La Globa* (founded in 1934) was the first and largest cooking society to be established in Vitoria counting one hundred members, followed by *El Rincón Amado* with thirty members. *Zaldibartxo* in near-by Sarria (1941) was actually founded by Vitoria citizens, while *Olarizu* (1948) is known for a rather religious and aristocratic membership. In the 1950s they were followed by *Zaldiaran* and *San Juan – La Globa* (both founded in 1953). Since 1988, there has existed a federation of popular societies in Vitoria called *Gasteizko Elkarteak*; it started with eight societies and has at present twenty-seven societies as members. The main aim of the organization is to help organize the *Fiesta de San Prudencia* which includes a *tamborrada*. Other activities include cooking competitions, wine tastings and the *Campeonato de Mus*, the famous Basque card game. Today there are 126 popular societies in Alava altogether (including cooking and other

13 Against the overall tendency of including women, in Bilbao *txokos* seem to remain almost exclusively male. Meritxell Alonso Cespedes reports that out of 45 *txokos* that she visited only two officially welcomed women as members. This seems to be confirmed by a report that was filed by the Diputación Foral de Vizcaya which investigated how many women participated in voluntary associations; it found that only 0.7 percent of all respondents said that they participated in a gastronomic society (Alonso Cespedes 1996, 121).

recreational societies). Half of them are in Vitoria alone. They are mainly located in the old part of the Basque capital. (Idroqilis 1994, 41)

In Navarre, the development of the *sociedades* followed the well-established cultural patterns of Basque settlements: more developed in the north and north-east and fizzling out or non-existent in the south of the region (Aguirre Franco 1983, 64). Most societies can be found in Pamplona (fifteen; most prominently among them, *Napardi* and *Txoko Pelotazale*), Tafalla (fourteen), Tudela (seven), Elizondo (five) and Alsasua (four). In contrast to Gipuzkoa and Bizkaia, the term *sociedades* in Navarre refers almost exclusively to cooking societies. The absence of women is also marked in most of Navarre's cooking societies.

At present the Basque Autonomous Community (Gipuzkoa, Bizkaia and Alava) counts 1,300 societies (Idroquilis 1994, 17) but there are many more in Navarre and other Spanish cities and regions, particularly in those locations where a significant number of Basques get together.[14] In 1981 the Basque newspaper *Deia* reported that 50,000 Basques were members of cooking societies. The same paper reported that in one particular Bizkaian seaside town, Lekeitio, around 80 percent of the male population attended a cooking society regularly. Today the cooking society has become a symbol of the Basque diaspora worldwide and *txokos* can be found in almost any major capital or city that has a significant number of Basques – from Buenos Aires to New York and London.

14 It should be noted here that around 150,000 Basques are living in Madrid. Not surprisingly one could not 'survive' in Spain's capital without having a proper *sociedad*, the *Txoko Zar* (founded in 1968).

4.2 Formal Organization, Social Context and Function of the *Txoko*

For a gastronomic society to function properly, basic institutional arrangements are necessary and some established rules have to be followed (Anton Idroqilis 1994, Alonso Cespedes 1996 and Luengo 2001) In 1964, the Franco regime relaxed its attitude vis-à-vis civil associations and organizations, and decided to introduce a new law of associations (*ley de asociaciones*) that was followed by a by-law in 1965,[15] specifying possible applications and interpretations. Under the new rules, each association or society had to state where the place or location of the association was, the reasons for, and purposes of its existence, the social environment the association or society appealed to, how its administrative organization was ordered, what the rules concerning membership and access were, and what rights and duties the members had. The society also had to declare its non-profit aims, and finally it had to specify the rules concerning its own possible dissolution. Furthermore, the society needed to be registered with the official register of associations of the Basque government, and on demand had to prove that it followed the rules in terms of official book-keeping, documentation, the designated regulations, and so on. The typical structure would involve a general assembly, whose members elect an executive committee consisting usually of six to eight people, depending on the size of the society. The executive committee usually consists of a president, a vice-president, a treasurer, a secretary, the head of infrastructure and sometimes a speaker (Anton Idroqilis 1994: 23ff).

Based on her research of cooking societies in present-day San Sebastián, Anke van Wijck (2001, 19ff) has found that apart from the original 'founding fathers', recruitment of new members is usually based on the recommendation of two members of a given society. Very often priority is given to the offspring of members. Membership usually requires that members are adults over twenty-one years old. Van Wijck also points out that there

15 Partly modified, these laws and by-laws remain valid to this day.

are different forms of membership. Apart from the permanent members one can also encounter honorary and transient members.

As both Anton Idroquilis (1994, 22ff) and van Wijck (2001, 19ff) have stressed, membership and membership recruitment still vary between societies, and remain a topic of some debate. Today very few societies have rules with regard to the official prohibition on women's membership or on the physical presence of women in the clubhouse. Customs seem to vary from town to town, and from province to province, being stricter for example in Alava and Navarre, and more liberal in Gipuzkoa and some parts of Bizkaia. Thus we find today very few societies who openly limit the membership exclusively to adult males. Most societies allow women to have either completely open access, or to enter at certain hours of the day. Some societies specify that women are not allowed in the kitchen or that they should always be accompanied by male members.[16] Anton Idroqilis (1994, 22) explains the early tradition of excluding women stemmed from the time when San Sebastián's *sidrerias* – the cider houses, the predecessors of the popular societies – were rarely frequented by women. Aguirre Franco (1983) and van Wijck (2001) relate the absence of women more to an old division of labour, that is, that fishing and artisan work were usually done by males and that men needed 'some space of their own'. Luengo (2001) provides a more functional explanation, pointing towards the fact that with increasing differentiation in modern society, particularly in terms of the division of labour and tasks – women can now increasingly be found in jobs that just a few decades ago were male only – Basque society also became more inclusive and welcoming towards women.

During the Franco years, the law of associations still demanded that the associations or societies abstained from politics. Today the contributions that societies and associations make to civil society are widely acknowledged. For example, the Basque Government encourages the founding of recreational and gastronomic societies by providing starting grants and

16 Reliable data are hard to come by. Anton Idroquilis (1994, 32) estimates for Alava and its capital Vitoria that today about 50 percent of all societies allow women to use the society without any restrictions.

contributing to building or modernizing expenses. It is now common to find society rules and regulations that specify – apart from the formal aspects – what the purpose and the 'rules of engagement' of each society are. Thus, in her study of such matters, Alonso Cespedes (1996) quotes from a sign that she encountered in a *txoko* in Bilbao that reminded its members '... to be generous in spirit, to keep the place clean and in proper order, don't be blasphemous, be humorous, make space and put things back where they belong, be welcoming and open to visitors and members, regard the association as if it were the artery of society, be moderate ...' (Alonso Cespedes 1996: 85ff).

Other societies are expressing their *raison d'être* in more humorous fashion. Thus, a painting in a society in Mutriku (Gipuzkoa province) shows a Basque man with a *txapela vasca*, a Basque beret, emptying a wine glass with the deeply meaningful inscription 'Si hay, hay. Si nohay, nohay.' (When there is, there is. When there is nothing, then there is nothing.) Against such minimalism in terms of the rules of engagement Anton Idroqilis (1994, 23ff) points out that, at least in the Basque province of Alava, it is still common in societies not to talk about politics or religion. Likewise, van Wijck (2001, 24) notes that the rules of *Euskal Billera*, one of the most renowned societies of San Sebastián, still contains the sentence that 'this society does not confess to any political ideology'. It is fair to say that such reminders are not necessarily a proof that all activities and discussions in a society are politics-free; it is merely a warning to members and guests not to be too dogmatic or to appear to be sermonizing.

The government-imposed legal framework only addresses minimal formalities and structural requirements of a given society. What is of course absolutely essential for a society to function is a proper infrastructure. A gastronomic society usually provides an infrastructure that resembles that of a restaurant. But unlike a restaurant, it is not open to the general public, but only to the society's members or their guests.[17] The arrangement

17 The most important member of the *sociedad* is the one who holds the general key. It is he who has to make sure that any member may, at his will, enter any time he wishes. Membership in cooking societies is inevitably limited and its numbers controlled by

between kitchen and eating-place is also different. The kitchen is usually open or half-open and not completely separated or out of sight, as is the case with restaurants. The cooking arrangements are such that they include everything necessary to prepare food for large groups: usually two or three ovens, including open fire-places or grills, cooking instruments, freezers and fridges. Some societies have more than one kitchen and more than one room for the preparation and consumption of food. Seating arrangements are such that larger groups sit at one – long, square or round – table; though one can also find smaller tables for smaller get-togethers.[18] A society also

---

the members. More often then not, numbers are limited due to the very restrictions of the locality itself. Membership fees are not exceptionally high, and the monthly contribution usually does not exceed 1 percent of the overall income of one earner. It is important to stress that members can bring as many friends as they like and as often as they like. On occasions there may be waiting lists for new members, particularly in those societies that have a good name or record.

The very fact that only members and their guests can enter the society distinguishes it from other public gathering places and establishments such as the more politically oriented *batzoki* or the *herriko tabernak*, which are open in principle to all those who identify with or give support to a certain political cause. In the case of the *batzoki* this would be people who support the party which has been following a traditional and conservative independence course, the Partido Nacionalista Vasco (PNV-EAJ) founded by Sabino Arana (who was also the first politician to suggest a *batzoki* in every Basque town and *barrio*); in the case of the *herriko tabernak* one would encounter rather those who sympathize with the radical *abertzale* (patriotic) movement of Herri Batasuna (now Batasuna) or one of its fellow organizations. By no means are these bars totally exclusive, and on occasions such as a *fiesta* one can find quite a broad mix of people from all kinds of political or non-political background and affiliation, including blow-ins or people from the neighbourhood who just happen to pop in for 'the one' or the last one, *el ultimo*.

18 It should be stressed here that usually not all members are present at the one time. The normal procedure is that members make a reservation in advance, that is, they put down their names and the expected number of eaters in the society's calendar or book-keeping journal. For smaller parties it is often not necessary to make reservations. In order to find out, members just have to check the reservation list. Very often individual members just use the society as a place to relax or to hang out, or to play games, or to have a drink with some other members. Food may or may not accompany such activities.

provides cleaning facilities, bathrooms and – most important – storage space, so that a stock of supplies which are regularly needed to prepare and to consume food can be stored (including the basics, such as salt, pepper, oil and a well-stocked *bodega* for wine as well). Most societies also have – apart from the wine cellar – full bar facilities, including coffee and espresso machines. The cooking itself is usually done on a voluntary basis and is almost always based on experience. Those members do the cooking who have a history of culinary excellence. The cook's expertise is often based on prior experience such as having cooked on a ship, at ceremonies or fiestas, and at a farmstead (*baserri*), and so on. The only acknowledgement of the cook's efforts may be a common toast or a word of thanks from other members and their guests.

After the meal is finished, usually at a time when the *digestivo* is being served, a bill is prepared and the members who enjoyed the meal have to pay *pro rata*. Since the basic infrastructure for consumption has been provided by the society, and since all the work (buying, preparing, cooking) has been done on an unpaid, voluntary basis, the bill is usually far below the price for an average restaurant meal, and is in fact probably even cheaper than a home-cooked meal. It is also worthwhile mentioning that most of the buying is done through well-established contacts: members of the society know local producers and buy directly from them, thus avoiding the market. Very often members of the society happen to be fishermen, or work in a *baserri* or know somebody who does, and thus sellers sometimes offer the basic ingredients such as fish and meat free, or at a much lower price than normal. Depending on individual expenses and buying procedures sometimes the bill is split, so that buyer-members can be reimbursed. The usual procedure, however, is that one pays *pro rata* and that the money thus collected goes – together with a detailed bill – into an envelope and is then posted through the internal mail system or is put into a cashbox, the *cajetín*, later to be collected by the financial secretary of the society. To get the sums right and to avoid errors is most important; as should have become from the description above, the entire system only works on the basis of trust and honesty.[19]

A society is based upon a certain legal framework and requires a physical location. But the *txoko* only comes to life because it is an institutional expression of a much larger social phenomenon, the *cuadrilla* (Arpal 1985; Ramirez Goikoetxea 1985). The *cuadrilla* is the result of a complex shift from a rural environment to urban structures. In order to understand the interaction between *txoko* and *cuadrilla* a detailed explanation is called for. One has first of all to understand the role that the street (*kalea*) plays in Basque culture. One has to distinguish between a rural and an urban form of social life in the Basque Country. (Arpal 1985, 132ff). In the countryside, we find the *etxea* (rural house or farmstead), which is agricultural and private in character; its social type is the *baserritarra*, the man or woman who lives the rural life. In this cultural context, rural life usually denotes being somehow 'closer to nature' and living in a natural environment that remains 'unspoiled' and thus virtuous. In contrast, urban life in the city or town is symbolized through the *kalea*, the street, which is by definition open to the public. Its main expression is the *kaletarra*, the man or woman who lives in the street. Life in an urban environment denotes 'civilization'. It is seen to be 'artificial', 'unnatural' and involving less-than-ideal aspects of city life such as alienation, indifference, social distance and anonymity.

Until the nineteenth century, the Basque Country only had some very limited urban development, and the typical town only had three streets:

19 The evidence of trust and honesty calls for a more detailed sociological explanation than I will be able to give here. One possible way of understanding the successful functioning of the *txoko* could be that of exchanging gifts and reciprocity patterns as explained in Marcel Mauss's famous study *The Gift* (1990). While on first impression it looks as if some members of cooking societies do more voluntary work than others (and do so sometimes repeatedly) a more equal and reciprocal system might actually be at work here. This becomes particularly clear when one studies cooking societies and their social environment over a longer time period. What the researcher can encounter is that in one way or another those who do more work in the cooking society (as providers of goods or services) eventually will receive a 'gift' in return. This can be in the form of a favour granted, a particular wish fulfilled, or in the form of a symbolic present.

the one above (*la de arriba* or *goikoa*), the middle street (*la de enmedio* or *erdikoa*) and the lower street (*la de abajo* or *behekoa*), and the houses along those streets (Arpal 1985, 132). Only three urban agglomerations, Bilbao, Vitoria and San Sebastián, developed into urban centres; but even in these cases the old quarters only had half a dozen streets, so that very often even the main square, the *plaza*, was outside the *casco viejo* (old town). Beyond the old town, other urban settlements (*ensanches*) only developed later. Very often, wealthier farmsteads included, apart from the free-standing main *baserria* in the countryside known as the *casa solar*, also a *casa en la calle*, a house in the town, so that in a sense the countryside often extended into town. This picture of the street in front of the farmstead (*baserria* or *caserío*) can be regarded as an expression of an ongoing conflict whereby some of the boundaries between countryside, village/town and city were blurred or still not clearly distinguished. Only with the turn of the twentieth century did the situation change. But even today, in a time where urban centres and urban life have come to dominate modern Basque society, one can still encounter many symbolic representations of rural life in most Basque towns and cities. Analysts have pointed towards a complex situation where symbolic transfers from a rural to an urban environment are still common (Arpal 1985, 135). Its symbol is the 'urban villager' who has emerged as a new social type and who combines elements of both *baserritarra* and *kaletarra*.

The urban villager's main social reference point is the *cuadrilla*, a social formation that is defined by certain common characteristics that the individuals who make up the group share: the same generational cohort, being of the same sex, or having played together in the same street or *barrio* (quarter) where one grew up. Crucial are those shared experiences or rites of passage that usually mark an individual for life, but which also help to form a collective memory that all of the group can refer to: prep-school, school, military service, important political events, and so on. It should be noted, however, that the function of the *cuadrilla* has evolved and changed over time. During the Franco years, and even during the transition to the new democratic polity, the *cuadrilla* provided a certain sort of stabilizing social infrastructure, a response on the behalf of civil society to an unstable political environment. As Pérez-Agote (1986) has pointed out, the *cuadrilla* established a kind of parallel world in which one could encounter aspects of life which both the Franco regime, and the particularly turbulent political transition in the Basque Country which followed Franco, could not provide. Such elements included trust, friendship, social contact, and equality in communication, and they provided a sense of stability in everyday life that was otherwise lacking (Pérez-Agote 1986, 105ff). However, the unique public response and the privatization of public life as in the case of the *cuadrilla* have also created a strange vacuum with respect to private life in the sense that the group's demand on an individual can also take its toll – that of not having enough private time (Pérez-Agote 1986, 128). Since Pérez-Agote made his comments in the mid-1980s, political tensions have somewhat eased.[20] Nonetheless, it must be stressed that not all of the political problems that caused such a unique constellation between the public and private sphere in the first place have disappeared, and until today one can discern a deep distrust in the Basque Country vis-à-vis 'official' political institutions and arrangements.

The sociologist Jesús Arpal (1985, 136ff) has provided us with a brief phenomenology of the life of a typical *cuadrilla* as it occurs today. The group, usually consisting of five to ten people, gets together to spend time and go to places – just as the political ritual described below demands. The group meets regularly for the *chiquiteo* or *poteo*, consisting of a round through the different bars of a specific zone or *barrio*, which is in most cities located in the *casco viejo*. This occurs in most cases almost daily, usually either before lunch or before dinner. It also happens on other occasions, following the calendar of festivities, or on birthdays and anniversaries. In many cases, the *poteo* has become part of a daily routine and seems to an outsider as being almost compulsive. In some cases the movement and appearances of some *cuadrillas* have become such an established pattern that the bartender does not need to hear the order anymore. Thus, just as the

20 Political tensions in the Basque Country peaked in the late 1970s when two referenda were held, one on the acceptance of the Spanish constitution and one that led to the creation of the present Basque Autonomous Community. Both led to heavy demands in terms of political activity, often involving entire *cuadrillas*.

cuadrilla leaves its mark on the vicinity, so too does the vicinity influence some of the group's habits.[21] However, one of the most interesting aspects of the *cuadrilla* phenomenon is that it does not impose unanimity; it is a collective phenomenon that leaves time and space for individual expression and creativity. As with any group, over time various roles evolve within the group, and leaders emerge who are more popular and acknowledged than others. In some cities and towns, they even have nick-names so popular that in some places they are only known by that name. In order to gain the respect of one's friends, it is crucial to be seen to remain 'authentic' and true to one's 'real' self. Thus, some members are known only by their unique appearance, character or apparently 'authentic' attitude or history.

Returning now to the key issue of the nature of cooking societies, *txokos* are manifestations of well-established social contacts, mainly (but not only) of the *cuadrilla* type.[22] The *txoko* and the social relations that it

21 It is a normal occurrence in modern urban life that not all people of the same *cuadrilla* remain in the town where they were born. Yet displacement does not mean the complete dispersion of the group. A core usually stays together and welcomes the 'displaced person' whenever he or she comes back. Usually the group also knows the 'rites of passage', i.e. when somebody says good-bye before committing him- or herself to a new, usually married life. Yet all group members also know that – apart from extreme circumstances – in most cases this is not a good-bye forever and that there will be 'comebacks' and reunions at the next *fiesta* or public celebration. It should be added here that *cuadrillas* can also radically change in terms of membership or even disband entirely. The former happens when there is a fresh injection of new blood, usually through marriage; occasionally friends introduce other friends who have just moved into town and, over time, these new members are then 'adopted' and incorporated. Alternatively *cuadrillas* can also disband or disappear altogether; this usually happens when the ties that bind have become too loose, be it through massive exit of individual members to another place or simply through death. However, most *cuadrillas* last an entire life-cycle, from early adolescence to old age. In small towns it is not unusual to see the surviving remains of a *cuadrilla*, some of them in their 80s, going out for the *poteo*.

22 Different stories and explanations emerge once the focus shifts from San Sebastián to the smaller towns and villages along the Cantabrian coast. Thus, Homobono tells us that in the case of Bermeo (Bizkaia), the historical connection between the *tripulación* (fishing crew), the *cofradía* (the fishermen's fraternity), the *cuadrilla* and

represents are a means to reconstitute the reciprocity of relations that have their origins in more traditional forms of life; yet they are essentially new in that they represent a modern form of social relations in a growing and increasingly influential urban environment. Originally a peculiar invention of San Sebastián's unique class constellation at the beginning of the twentieth century, the popular societies in general, and the gastronomic societies in particular, have over the course of a century, become less class-based and are now more inclusive and more explicable as inter-class phenomena than ever before (Luengo 2001, Arpal 1985).

4.3 Between Homogenization and Differentiation: Basque Cooking and Culinary Culture

Having examined the history and micro-level operations of the cooking societies, I will now look at some broader issues, namely the ways in which cooking, eating and drinking together in the *txoko* are linked to some of the region's physical, cultural and historical features. It is impossible to discuss

---

the *txoko* is much stronger and more continuous than in the case of San Sebastián. (Homobono 1987, 314ff). In Bermeo common eating was originally organized by the *cofradía* as a symbolic expression of renewing contracts; its function was to bind together the crew *(tripulación)* that went out to the risky and dangerous sea together. The common banquet for the *tripulación* that had been organized by the *cofradía* became less and less frequent and was abolished around the turn of the century. Also, as the strong *tripulación* ties weakened and gave way to the social life of the *cuadrilla* – a differentiation process in terms of separating work and leisure activities was mainly responsible for that – the ritual was increasingly replaced by two other habits: the common drink in the *loije*, a tavern that was usually close to the landing place or *muelle*, and the common meal of the *cuadrilla* in the *txoko*. However, Homobono also found in his study that although the *txoko* remains an option, particularly during one of the most important local fiestas, eating out, i.e. opting for a restaurant, is becoming more and more popular, particularly amongst women (Homobono 1987, 354).

social aspects of the *txoko* such as conviviality and commensality, without combining the question of 'what do the members actually eat and what do they drink when they are together?' with the historical–geographical question of 'why particularly in the Basque Country?' In comparison to eating and drinking together, there is no other human activity in which function and content are so closely associated with, and dependent on, each other.[23] Form is indeed condensed substance, and in order to appreciate

23 This cannot be the place to discuss all the pros and cons of structuralist explanations. However, if one applies Claude Lévi-Strauss's famous matrix of the raw, the cooked and the rotten to Basque alimentation, food preparation and eating habits, no clear picture emerges. It is, for example, not clear whether the boiled is closer to 'endo-cooking' (more intimate groups like the family) while roasted food is closer to 'exo-cooking' (more open, public consumption) as the famous model suggests. Particularly the fact that a popular institution like the *txoko* mixes aspects of the private and the public makes Lévi-Strauss's concept almost impossible to apply. Defenders of Lévi-Strauss concede that many ethnic, regional or national cuisines mix various forms of food-preparation. Nevertheless, they still argue that distinctions of food preparation can be made and that particularly the roasted/boiled opposition – the main part of the structuralist matrix – remains valid.

In his study of *Basque Cooking: History and Preparation*, Busca Isusi (1987, 9, 105), one of the most renowned Basque commentators and experts, has stressed that with the exception of oysters and clams, eating raw ingredients is not common in the Basque Country. As to the argument of 'the raw', almost every other form of food conservation and food preparation is being applied. Very often – and this goes against the core of the structuralist argument – the natural material or ingredient that is being used does not change but the method of preparing it does. Furthermore, when it comes to such methods as smoking, grilling, frying, marinating, drying, steaming, baking and braising, there is no evidence that the structuralist explanation applies. In contrast and more often than not, the methods of preparation depend on seasonal circumstances and availability, individual taste and common decisions, habits or religious customs and traditions. To speak of a religious calendar as a structure would make little sense to hard-core structuralists. It should also be pointed out that between available material and preparation there are occasionally 'no-do' rules, but these seem to have to do more with the fact that one does not want to destroy or waste food.

One could of course ridicule the structuralist argument by pointing out that there is clear evidence from the excavations of pre-historic sites such as Santimamiñe and

fully the formal aspects of eating together in the cooking society it is necessary to refer at least briefly to the history of alimentation, nutrition and cooking – in short, the content – which in turn is often linked to unique historical-geographical patterns in the Basque Country.

In general terms and historically speaking, Basque cooking has always followed the old division between the Atlantic North and the Mediterranean South (Iturbe and Letamendia 2000: 12ff). In the Atlantic zone, developed forms of agriculture were always limited, mainly because of its rugged terrain and humid climate. Fishing is omnipresent, and the supply of meat and fat usually comes from farm animals such as chickens, goats, lambs and cows. In terms of alcoholic drinks, apple cider and some white wine (*txakoli* from microclimates and *terroirs* such as in Getaria, Gipuzkoa) are the norm. In contrast, the southern zone has a rather dry climate, and a less rugged, more extensive and farmable terrain that allows for the development of sophisticated forms of agriculture, such as asparagus, spinach, artichokes, and cereals. Inland, large-scale farming and a cattle industry developed. In terms of nutritional models and cuisine, the fat is not animal-derived but comes mainly from olives. Also in contrast to the Atlantic zone, in the south sophisticated wine making developed, especially in parts of Alava and Navarre. The different geographical patterns explain the availability and the peculiar choice of food in the *txokos* of each zone or region. We can thus encounter an omnipresence of fish and seafood in the Atlantic zone while meat and vegetables are more likely to make it onto the menu in

---

Ekain that the first Basques ate oysters and that the rest of the historical development of alimentation in the Basque Country is just a variation of some structure that developed thousands of years ago (Haranburu Altuna 2000, 21–24). Such an argument would miss the crucial point, namely that of evolution and historical novelty (such as the discovery of America and its impact on alimentation).

However, Busca Icusi discovers some structure in terms of distinctions between men and women when it comes to meat preparation. He writes: 'At present, the gastronomic societies of predominatly male membership are the ones in which the preparation of meats is best known, given that the feminine presence is often not well received. Women prefer to stew and bake than roast or grill. The persistence of recipes for roasted meats in largely masculine cooking is noteworthy' (Busca Icusi 1987, 9).

the southern zone such as Alava and Navarre. Equally, the choice of wine is particular to each zone or region, *txakoli* from Getaria or white wine from Galicia are more likely to be consumed in *txokos* located in coastal communities, while the top-rank red Riojas or the best Navarre wines are more likely to be consumed where they have been produced.[24]

Over time three main influences have changed food consumption patterns in the Basque Country. First, there was a radical change in terms of alimentation through the discovery of America and the introduction of American produce such as corn, potato, pepper, tomato, beans, sugar and chocolate to both the northern and southern zones. The introduction of corn, beans and the potato were especially influential on nutritional patterns (Iturbe and Letamendia 2000, 50ff, Haranburu Altuna 2000, 161f, Busca Isusi 1987, 13–17)

The second most important influence was that of the Catholic Church. It established a religious calendar, which served as a guide prescribing what to avoid or what to eat at which particular time. (Iturbe and Letamendia 2000, 53ff; Haranburu Altuna 2000, 118–165, 201–202) Religious abstinence demanded non-eating of meat, meat soup, eggs, milk products or animal fat. Days of abstention were Wednesdays and Fridays and additionally other selected days during the year. Thus, for the remaining days of the year fish provided the alternative. Today, Basque society and culture are much more secularized. However, secularization does not mean that old consumption habits stemming from a Catholic background have completely disappeared. It is still the tradition in many household-kitchens and *txokos* to provide fish or seafood around Christmas and the New Year, while some days of the *fiesta* demand meat days and related dishes. The calendar of festivity days is full of days for saints, which demand a certain form of cooking. Additionally there are birthdays, weddings, retirements,

24 Having stressed some regional pattern to food and alcohol consumption, this should not lead to the wrong conclusion that these patterns are exclusive. Nobody likes monotony when it comes to food and drink and the same applies to the Basque Country. Furthermore, improved transport, refrigeration and short distances have made it possible that fresh produce, be it from either the southern zone or from the Atlantic zone, are now easily available wherever one cooks.

stag nights and funerals, events which themselves usually determine the choice of what to eat and drink. However, the Catholic Church emphasized and actively promoted communitarian habits of eating, and not only in the case of such special events; eating together was also a measure against the threat of Protestant individualism. Eventually, eating together, religious belief and social life developed into a custom, as can be seen in that institutional microcosm that is the *txoko*.

The third influential impact on eating habits and food consumption came with the modernization of Basque society at the turn of the century. Particularly important were the development of a modern infrastructure (installation and improvement of rail and road networks) and the development of the means of communication (telegraph, telephone, and later radio and film). Such improvements helped a modern tourist industry to emerge. Taken together with industrialization, they resulted in the creation of an urban, industrialized environment and culture. An immediate result of such changes was a new landscape of political cultures. While the liberals favoured the newly emerging rationalized form of urban culture, particularly in Bilbao and San Sebastián, the traditional rural way of life saw itself besieged by modernization and rationalization processes (Iturbe and Letamendia 2000, 59ff). The conflict between the two opposing forces finally gave way to a new, third force – Basque nationalism. Basque nationalism had a particular impact on the cuisine and food patterns because it combined aspects of both conservatism and modernization. As Basque nationalism aimed at the reconstruction of what it means to be Basque, it paid considerable attention to such symbolic capital as food and eating together (Iturbe and Letamendia 2000, 62).[25]

25 The founder of modern Basque nationalism, Sabino Arana Goiri, had been arrested by the Spanish authorities and had to spend time in prison (August 1895 to January 1896; the reason given for his arrest was that he had sent a telegram to the President of the United States congratulating him on the liberation of Cuba from Spain). He knew how to celebrate when Christmas came. His sister prepared him a fine meal and delivered it to his prison cell. As a starter he had olives and anchovies, for the main course oysters, soup, cod in red sauce, sea-bass and fried hake, followed by apple compote and a selection of other delicious sweets. The meal was accompanied by

The traditional style of rural food preparation and consumption,[26] the urban standardization of cooking in such places as hotels and restaurants, together with the nationalist attempt at reconstructing culinary symbolic capital, all contributed to producing a new common cuisine for which the new label *cocina vasca* truly applied and of which *txoko* cooking has become an institutional expression. As one observer commented, what is so remarkable about this new constellation was the coming together of two processes, that of a homogenization and that of a differentiation process (Haranburu Altuna 2000, 299ff). The homogenization process is clearly visible in the 'Mediterraneanization' of food in the Basque Country, with the 'olive-based' alimentation of the Ebro valley reaching the Cantabrian coast and being now omnipresent in the Atlantic provinces of Gipuzkoa and Bizkaia. At the same time modern transportation and food preservation

---

fine wines and ports, among them a white *txakoli* from Getaria. (The details stem from Ceferino Jemein's biography of Sabino Arana and are referred to in Haranburu Altuna 2000, 257f.)

It should be mentioned here that Arana wasn't the first intellectual to distinguish between Basque and other food. The distinction of food *de aqui* and *de fuera* is much older and probably goes back to a proto-nationalist argument that can be found in the work of a Basque Jesuit from Azpeitia, Padre Larramendi, *Corografia de Guipúzkoa* (written in 1754, published 1882). Larramendi's influence is discussed in Haranburu Altuna, 2000, 214–220.

26 Various cooking books and recipes of Basque cuisine had been published in the nineteenth century (*Escualdun Cocinera*, Bayona 1864 and *Cocinan ikasteko liburua*, Tolosa 1889). However, it was only with the publication of cooking books from two particular restaurants which helped to develop the term *cocina vasca*. *El Amparo* was a legendary restaurant in Bilbao; it opened its doors in 1886 and but had to close in 1918 due to the death of one of the two inheritors. The first edition of its most famous recipes, *El Amparo: sus platos clasicos*, appeared in 1930. The second most famous cooking book stemmed from a San Sebastián restaurant, *La Nicolasa*. Its recipes were published (under the same name and title) in 1935. Both books helped to name and define those dishes which are now considered to be classical Basque dishes. In the name of historical justice we should add a third title, which did not have its origins in a restaurant but nevertheless helped to define seafood and fish culture as it exists today in the Basque Country: *El libro del pescado*, published by Imanol Baleak in 1933. For more information on the three titles see Haranburu Altuna 2000, 260–268.

made it possible that the fresh fruits and fish of the Atlantic now reach Navarre and Alava – to such an extent that they are now considered to be a part of the staple diet. However, such homogenization has not led to total monotony or dominance; there always existed and continues to exist a variety and diversity in the regions – to such an extent that some have called for the change of the label *cocina vasca* to *cocinas vascas* in the plural to reflect regional differentiation (Haranburu Altuna, 301).

With regard to the development of alimentation and cooking over the last twenty years, modernization and rationalization processes have culminated in what has been called the new Basque cuisine – *la nueva cocina vasca*. The development of the new Basque cuisine can be interpreted as a critique of the rationalization process as it has developed so far. Against what could be called a certain saturation and stagnation process – food preparation and presentation had remained unchanged and there was hardly anything new, adventurous or surprising about the standard menu – this new movement called for a general overhaul. The new movement demanded a return to the culinary 'basics'; at the same time it demanded also that the produce be fresh. The avant-garde of this culinary revolution consisted mainly of innovative restaurant chefs and cooking society experts (and very often these roles can overlap in the Basque Country).[27] The history of the new Basque cuisine has been truly revolutionary and has been so successful that today most of the more sophisticated Basque restaurants and *txokos* have incorporated its demands. Throughout the year there are now numerous competitions in the Basque Country in which *txoko* cooks – mainly during the fiestas but by no means limited to them – contribute to

27 The famous ten commandments of the movement include: 1. a rejection of unnecessary and useless complications and a return to natural produce, 2. a call for the reduction of cooking time, 3. practising the cuisine of the market, 4. reducing the offer of menus on the card and adapting to what the local cuisine can freshly provide, 5. abolishing sauces and other dressings, 6. simplifying the sauces and using sauces only to support the natural taste, 7. a return to the regional and autochthon gastronomy, 8. the incorporation and application of new techniques, 9. the promotion of a cuisine that is healthy, 10. supporting creativity and inventiveness with the aim of creating new dishes. (C. Millau, quoted in Haranburu Altuna 2000, 294).

the development of Basque cooking in the directions of further innovation and sophistication. They are helped by thousands of *txoko* members and guests who all think that they would not enjoy the *cocina vasca* if cooking and eating were isolated or solitary affairs.

4.4 Reluctant Modernization III: 'Commensality', 'Loyalty' and Urban Forms of Life

In his writings on late eighteenth century England, E. P. Thompson (1980, 1991) suggested that plebeian culture and moral economy are intrinsically linked. 'Plebeian culture' was an auxiliary term that Thompson used to describe a situation where class was not what classic Marxist theory assumed it to be. Rather than forming nascent prototypes of the industrial working class, Thompson preferred to see classes in terms of fields of gravity, that is, as heterogeneous constellations consisting of many dimensions and layers and in which traditional popular customs played a major role. It was these common customs that also helped to keep a moral economy alive – an economy which could take on various and different meanings for the plebeian crowds – such as common rights, norms or obligations, day-to-day habits, customs and practices but which, taken together, in many ways constituted a force that was alien and opposed to the power elite. Furthermore, and more to the point of peculiarly Basque conditions, any closer look into the stratification structure of the Basque Country will reveal that, apart from the metropolitan region of Bilbao, its industrial environs, and a few industrial towns and industrial development zones such as Durango, Eibar, Elgoibar, Ermua and Hernani, clear-cut, visible class structures can hardly be encountered. In many ways the Basque Country seems to be a prime illustration of Thompson's main notion of plebeian culture. Indeed, the work of social historians and historical anthropologists that I have repeatedly referred to here, such as Luengo (2002), Homobono (1987, 1989, 1990, 1997) and Arpal (1985), confirms the existence of such a plebeian cultural macro-constellation and the place cooking societies play in its moral economy.

While historians and social scientists have hinted at the macro-constellations such as plebeian cultures and the moral economy that go with them, the political economist Albert O. Hirschman has looked at so-called micro-constellations by which he mainly meant institutional dimensions. In *Passions and the Interests* (1977) he first hinted at the possibility that in the modern age passions and interests are much more intrinsically linked than has often been assumed. Concepts derived from his approach to moral economy, particularly the idea of 'commensality' (Hirschman 1998: 11–32), allow the researcher to take a closer look at the micro-level and the peculiar links that exist between the public and the private sphere and between customs and morals (Hess, 1999).

In his seminal book *Shifting Involvements: Private Interest and Public Action* (1982), Hirschman addressed the problem of periodic shifts that have occurred in modern civil society. In this work he analysed both the retreat into privacy and the inclination towards public action in wave-like appearances. The main motive behind both private retreat and public action was then a sense of disappointment. At this time Hirschman did not discuss social practices in which public concern mingles with private activities and thereby helps to maintain a civic equilibrium in civil society. To go a step further, merging the two spheres, the private and the public, was regarded as a potential threat to civil society. However, in the essay about commensality that Hirschman wrote much later, and in which he revisits some of his previous arguments, he asks us to think about occasions where the merging of the two spheres can actually have positive results. Hirschman now points out that 'economists [and other social scientists] have often looked at the consumption of food as a purely private and self-centreed activity' (Hirschman 1998, 28). Hirschman continues his argument by stressing that social scientists usually forget about other dimensions:

> While they are consuming food and drink, people gathering for the Mahlzeit engage in conversation and discussion, exchange information and points of view, tell stories, perform religious services, and so on. From the purely biological point of view, there is no doubt that eating has a straightforward relationship to individual welfare. But

> once they are done in common, eating and drinking normally go hand in hand with a remarkably diverse set of public or collective activities (ibid., 29).

Hirschman further stresses that the function of the common meal of commensality can, and does indeed, vary. He reminds us in particular of Heinrich Mann's novel *Der Untertan* (*The Subject*) in which the main character Diederich Hessling is drawn into a form of beer drinking and pretzel eating commensality that can only be described as reactionary in terms of the later outcome, National Socialism. Against such negative examples and experiences, Hirschman reveals now the great potential of commensality, that is, non-means but ends-oriented interaction. It is exactly at this juncture that the Basque cooking society comes in. It seems to me that in the case of the *txoko* we are dealing with a positive example of how commensality – at least when organized collectively and when sensibly institutionalized – can have a positive function in providing loyalty through commensality and contributing to the maintenance of a civic equilibrium in society. In other words, when such commensality emerges, human beings are not treated just as means towards certain ends but as ends in themselves.

Providing the micro-institutional framework for such ends-centred interaction, the *txoko* contributes to the maintenance of the social equilibrium. *Txokos* are an institutionalized measure and increasingly an inter-class phenomenon against the divisions of modern society, or, in other words, an attempt at life-world integration (Luengo 2001; Arpal 1985; Habermas 1962). Located somewhere between tradition and modernity, they are attempts to provide answers to purely instrumental and systemic rationalization or system integration. However, in contrast to the roles of public institutions and the public sphere that Habermas emphasizes and promotes, *txokos* are neither purely public nor purely private institutions; rather they occupy a unique space somewhere in the middle of the continuum between the public and the private sphere. It is this very middle position which contributes to the *txokos'* success and popularity.

Yet one must also note that the *txoko* has not only 'progressive' social functions; it also reproduces existing age and sex/gender constellations, and often treats societal aspects as if they were community aspects (Arpal 1985, 140ff). In this context, some commentators have interpreted the *txoko* as a communal institution that functions as a compensation device by exercising a 'cooling' effect on an over-heated personality type and lessening tensions in a collective group therapy, almost resembling a psycho-dramatic setting. This interpretation suggests that the *txoko* provides a communal escape route from the grindings of societal life, implicitly suggesting a shift towards a communal 'exit' strategy and thus somehow limiting the positive impact on society as a whole (Aguirre Franco 1983 and van Wijck 2001).

However, it would be wrong to perceive the nature of the *txoko* solely in light of such extreme formulations. As an institution it is as good (or as bad) as the society and the members who constitute it. The fact remains that eating at the *txoko*, particularly during the fiestas, interrupts daily life and routine, and is clearly an expression of what Simmel has termed 'conviviality' (Homobono 1987). The *txoko* as an institution is also a symbolic reproduction of Basque society and identity and particularly supportive in terms of accommodating the transition from rural to urban life and thus providing an example of a historic reformulation of the community-society divide (Arpal 1985). As a potential reproduction cell for nationalist discourse, *cuadrilla* and *txoko* together can also be seen as nationalist models of sociability and commensality which are not bound by rigid class structures but rather bridge across class distinctions and positions (Pérez-Agote 1987, Luengo 2001).

Whatever the details and the individual and collective enjoyments in the *sociedades* are, it is obvious that this institution has indeed become a backbone of modern Basque society.[28] Against the disastrous experiences with certain forms of collectivity in both the former Soviet Union and

28 This statement does not neglect or contradict the fact that the Basque Country is also riddled by a major political conflict about the pros and cons of the project of self-determination and/or independence which over the last forty years had led to many casualties and victims. However, to derive from this fact that the Basque Country has in modern time been anywhere close to open civil war would be misleading and a seriously mistaken and a very one-sided view of the matter. It has been part of the complexities of the conflict that the commensality of the *txoko* and the killing of political opponents co-existed at the same time (although never or extremely rarely in the same place).

Nazi Germany (particularly when we think about totalitarianism as social and political regimes that tried to get rid of the private–public distinction), here, in the example of the Basque cooking societies, we find a form in which the public and the private actually enrich each other. It seems indeed wrong to degrade them as part of an invented tradition (Hobsbawm and Ranger, 1983) or regard them even as some sort of radical nationalist recruitment cells as is sometimes implicitly suggested by commentators like Juaristi (1987). The opposite is true: the *sociedades gastronómicas* are relatively modern institutions, which actually allow the Basque Country to overcome some of the tensions that arise when an old civilization meets the modern conditions of the twenty-first century. The relationship between the private and the public is a delicate one, and has not always worked out well in modern times. The *txoko*, which uniquely connects both spheres, appears to be indeed the Basques' most genuine and beneficial contribution to the question of how a plebeian culture with a long history can survive under modern conditions.

CHAPTER 5

Conclusion: Reluctant Modernization, Plebeian Culture and Moral Economy in the Basque Country

The term modernization connotes a complex development, a process that in some Western European countries and regions lasted for more than three centuries. Its main feature is the transformation of predominantly rural world and small communities into an urban and industrialized society. The modern order is furthermore distinguished from the old one in that producing for the market has become central, technology and science occupy a prominent position, and a political pluralist system represents many interests and allows for modern forms of democracy. The rationalization process of thought and action that accompanies this modernization appears as one in which instrumental means-ends thinking becomes dominant (van der Loo and van Reijen 1992, 11ff).

In order to understand the modernization and rationalization process, sociologists such as Ferdinand Tönnies and Emile Durkheim have designed oppositional ideal types, one that stands for the time prior to modernization and another one for the preliminary 'end product'. For Tönnies the term community equals family life, unity, 'Volk', communal and rural life, non-differentiated urban life, religion, church, household economy, and agricultural production. In contrast, society connotes urban and metropolitan life, state-oriented politics, cosmopolitan orientation, public discourse, trade, industry and the emergence of a scientific world (Tönnies 1887/1935, Hess 2001, 47). Similar notions led Emile Durkheim to distinguish between mechanical and organic solidarity (Durkheim 1893/1984, Hess 2001, 38f). Mechanical solidarity was the cement that bound primitive societies together; such societies or communities were marked by little or no division of labour, economically self-sufficient units and controlling, rather repressive forms of law, all of which left little or no room for individualist forms of life. In contrast, modern societies are held together by organic solidarity with a differentiated division of labour, the development and internalization of norms, and individualist life-styles. There were other, more processual dimensions that sociologists referred to when studying modernization. Max Weber, for example, described and interpreted the rationalizing process that marked the transition from the old to the modern order as a process of growing rationalization and disenchantment where instrumental rationality was dominant (Weber 1922/1968 and 1946).

Despite such critical reflections, it would take another half century before Talcott Parsons made the attempt to synthesize these classical sociological formulations and ideas and turned them into one coherent modernization approach. For Parsons, American society in particular had become the paradigm of successful modernization (Parsons 1971, Hess 2001, 120ff). In his view, earlier sociological conceptualizations provided important insights but in order to provide a coherent and comprehensive account of modernization Tönnies's, Durkheim's and Weber's concepts needed to be amalgamated. The net result was that the various differentiations and features that the classics had referred to were relegated in Parsons's systems approach. The various dimensions became subsystems and sub-functions, all of which contributed to the maintenance and equilibrium of modern society. By rendering and integrating crucial historical and present distinctions into a new overall framework, concrete history became if not abolished, then at least almost meaningless. Anything that appeared peculiar or exceptional or that somehow diverged from the great systems model was suspiciously regarded as being anti-modern, standing in the way or as simply being dysfunctional. In a bizarre and almost ironic way Parsons's grand theory design, which originally intended to address the issue of complexity, became synonymous with a rather narrow vision of what modernization was all about.

Critics like Barrington Moore immediately recognized that modernization did not come in one size and shape only. In his attempt to historicize the complex modernization process, Moore developed a three-path model in which predominantly agrarian societies managed to embark on a transformation process and finally arrived in modern industrial times (Moore 1966). The first route taken was that where the end product became known as Western democratic society. The examples that Moore referred to were the United States, France and the United Kingdom. All three had experienced an early bourgeois revolution and had managed to enter the industrialization process by the beginning of the nineteenth century and were firmly on track by the middle of the century. Because of the early bourgeois revolution the three countries managed to give their citizens – and that includes the masses of farmers and peasants – a voice and integrate them, while at the same time reducing the influence of the traditional rural sector by embarking on the process of industrial revolution. The second path that was taken resulted in modern fascism. Germany, Italy and to a certain extent Japan opted for this route. It ended in fascism mainly because the three countries did not have a successful early bourgeois revolution or a revolution of lasting impact. The traditional rural sector managed to remain influential, penetrating the political elites and influencing if not determining the politics of the three countries. Modernization was blocked for a long time, and when it came it took on an antidemocratic, radical and violent form, resulting in massive destruction – mainly because of older contradictions which fascism was never capable of solving. Lastly, there was the third road to modernization, that which ended up in communism. This route was taken by the former Soviet Union and somewhat later by China. Peasants remained an influential factor, one that could only be replaced by enforced industrialization from above – with either the state or the communist party apparatus as the main designers. In both cases it meant resorting to violent and oppressive means with the end result of no lasting democratic achievement.

In his groundbreaking study Barrington Moore was the first one to hint at the paradoxical and contradictory forms of the modernization process. Moore was soon to be joined by other critics such as E. P. Thompson. Like Moore, Thompson criticized the hidden sociological metaphysics of the structural functionalist approach of Talcott Parsons and Neil Smelser and the way they described the historical process of modernization (Thompson 1987, 238ff and 267ff). Pointing out that 'history knows no regular verbs', he reminded social theorists and sociologists that history has never been a process without a subject in which human agency, moral problems and ambiguous decisions simply disappeared or became buried in structures or differentiation processes. It is worthwhile quoting Thompson's polemic against Smelser, a Parsons scholar, here at length:

> Systems and sub-systems, elements and structures, are drilled up and down the pages pretending to be people. Smelser is anxious to show that social process occurred rationally an in an approved Parsonian fashion. There is a self-regulating social system (whose wisdom always appears most apparent if you happen to be at the top of it), 'governed' by a value-system (which, again, is enshrined in the institutions and attitudes of the system's governors), directed to goals legitimized by this value-system, which, when any major element within it differentiates structurally is precipitated into disequilibrium, resulting in dissatisfactions (always grossly misunderstood by those at the bottom, who, when they suffer, manifest, 'negative emotional reactions' and 'unjustified disturbance symptoms') but even these plebeian manifestations or irrationality the system is able to turn to functional account, since various superior non-economic 'elements' somewhere at the top of the system (such as 'political arrangements' or superior religious values or more simply the army and police) 'handle and channel' these disturbance symptoms, and, if the system's organs should flash out a 'justified' signal, devise, through several refined 'steps', 'new ideas' or institutions (which however are always devised in forms more wise than those agitated for by the deluded sources of disturbance) – thereby bringing to the structurally-differentiated 'system' a glorious return in 'an extraordinary growth of production, capitalization and profits' which, however, in the end falls short of the goals prescribed by the dominative value-system, thereby producing new dissatisfactions which in turn… I don't know how to extricate myself from this sentence, since the Parsonian system has indeed unlocked the secret of perpetual motion. (Thompson 1978, 267f)

Thompson himself also tried to practise what he taught. His own studies, assembled in *Customs in Common* (1991), show how one can study transitional, complex periods without falling into the traps of progressive periodizations either of systems theory or the Marxian type. In *Customs in Common* one sees Thompson constantly to-ing and fro-ing, always balancing the wealth of empirical material and the conceptual framework, one always informing the other and vice versa. What emerges in the end are 'thick descriptions' of a complex transition and modernization process, which was neither smooth nor developed 'organically'.

Like E. P. Thompson, Albert O. Hirschman also disliked the contradiction-free, almost 'smooth' description of the modernization process. That modernization did not evolve that smoothly or so contradiction-free, is revealed in Hirschman's study *Rhetoric of Reaction*, where he pointed out that modernization never was a straightforward unilinear process but that it was instead a paradoxical, uneven process that included major historical digressions and detours. For Hirschman the road to modernity was full of ambiguities, contradictions, ambivalences and often even outright resistance (Hirschman 1991, Hess 1999, 350ff). Taking a look at the various commentators who have accompanied and commented on the long journey towards modernity he distinguishes three approaches. The first approach is one in which normal meaning is turned upside-down and any reform project is rejected. Any expressed desire for improvement can only lead to worsening the present condition or state. The anti-modernist thinkers are aware of human limitations and unforeseen circumstances, but what appears at first sight to provide genuine insight into the human condition is in the end rendered completely meaningless because the idea that there can be anything new in this world is simply dismissed. The second approach Hirschman criticizes is similar to the first one but has an additional critical edge in the sense that it is assumed that underlying social structures have always been beyond the reach of collective human action, and that throughout history it has only been a small elite that made the far-reaching decisions while the masses only followed. To change these eternal conditions and iron laws would be futile. What this approach denies is the existence of any form of meaningful collective agency and subjectivity. The third approach that is subject to Hirschman's criticism argues that change can only threaten what has already been achieved. Here, past reforms are being played out against new ones. That increased democracy threatens an already achieved liberty is one of the standard complaints of this peculiar form of status-quo-defending, reactionary rhetoric.

Hirschman is concerned that all three forms of the rhetoric of reaction limit our understanding and possible vision of what has been and what is still possible and within human capacity and capability for change. Only by changing perspectives and keeping the lines of communication open between what often seem to be contradicting messages will we be able to conceive of the ambiguities, contradictions and ambivalences of the process of modernization.

We have seen how thinking about modernization started out first with descriptions of ideal types (Durkheim, Tönnies, Weber). These sociological classics were then deconstructed and re-interpreted by a new generation of system thinkers who argued that modernization was a unilinear and progressive paradigm and process (Parsons, Smelser). Against such clinical and contradiction-free attempts Moore, Thompson and Hirschman have voiced their concern and criticism. To these names we can add one other pioneering attempt to conceive of tradition and modernity differently, that of Joseph R. Gusfield. Referring to and reflecting on twentieth century India and other Asian experiences, Gusfield argues that it is plainly wrong to conceive of tradition and modernity as polar opposites in the linear theory of social change (Gusfield 1967). He also dismisses the presuppositions that there is a track leading to success called 'rational economic behaviour' and a final aim called modernity to which all roads lead as being plainly one-dimensional. In contrast to such claims, Gusfield points out that the experiences of new nations such as India have clearly shown that the old and the new, tradition and modernity, are much more entwined than had been previously thought. It is by no means always the case that the old is completely replaced by the new. Instead, mixed forms or fusion models encompassing the old and the new can regularly be encountered. Furthermore, the development of new practices, norms and values are by no means limited to what he calls the 'great tradition' of urban areas and cities (ibid., 353). The 'little tradition' of rural small town and villages can equally develop norms and values, particularly when new modern circumstances demand some form of adjustment. Traditional skills can be used and applied to pursue new ends, a selection of traditional values and norms can easily sit beside new values and norms, extended families, traditional trust and obligation can also supplement and help to get over the birth pangs of modern industrialized society. In short, 'tradition and modernity are frequently mutually reinforcing, rather than systems in conflict' (356). Gusfield also hints at the creative element when tradition is combined and applied to new circumstances and situations. New forms of nationalism might be an outcome of such combinations and fusion of old and new, tradition and modernity (359).

In his critique Gusfield refers mainly to the experience and examples such as India, where out of an old civilization and various traditional local cultures emerges a new nation. However, Gusfield's critique of a one-dimensionally perceived modernization process can also be applied to the history of multiple speeds and experiences of various western roads to nationhood, and it can help to fine-tune crucial arguments concerning modernization such as creative fusion and the mixing of traditional and modern elements.

As I have tried to explain throughout this book, the Basque Country is a case study which illuminates and illustrates most of the points raised above. With particular reference to three institutions – *baserri*, *cofradía* and *txoko* – I have tried to show how the Basques have been modernizers for a long time. To be more precise, they have been reluctant modernizers in the light of hegemonic, top-down modernizing attempts by their fellow countrymen, but they were modernizers nevertheless. More specifically, the present case study reveals three modes of adjusting to changing circumstances, two of them (*baserri* and *cofradía*) were successful for centuries but are now in terminal decline or already history, and one which is less old (the *txoko*) but which remains very much alive and finds itself in a healthy condition, actually to such an extent that it can be labelled a success story.

The three modes of reluctant modernization I called (after Albert O. Hirschman) 'exit', 'voice' and 'loyalty'. I have tried to see them also as expressions of a plebeian culture and an emerging moral economy (after E. P. Thompson). To be sure, the three modes of exit, voice and loyalty do not each appear exclusively and on their own, neither in the *baserria*, nor in the *cofradía* nor in the case of the *txoko*. As a matter of fact, all three institutions are institutions where all three modes can be encountered. However, historically speaking, in each institution one mode prevailed over the others in the end. As we have seen, 'exit' conditions were the main mode that prevailed and dominated in the *baserria*. The extended families of the *baserria* created a loyal core and managed to institutionalize a moral economy. The 'voice' option in the *baserria* remained structurally limited and in the end massive 'exit' from the farm and the rural world prevailed, leading to an institutional crisis – partly enforced through outside factors – from which the *baserria* would never recover. In the case of the *cofradía* the situation was different. Creating a 'voice' option for all the fishermen lies at the heart of the *cofradía*. For centuries the unique working environment that is the sea has helped to create this institutionalized form of 'loyalty'. This only functioned as long as the institution remained balanced, in the sense that the internal differentiation of labour and capital remained limited. Once modern market forces arrived (mainly in the form of modern trawling and the internationalization of the fish market), bringing a qualitative change to working and sales practices, the *cofradía* in its traditional form steered into crisis. To be sure, the *cofradía* managed to mix the old with the new for almost another century but has, towards the end of the twentieth century, really become defunct and is now moribund. The *txoko*, in contrast, remains the most successful institutional form in which an older plebeian culture and moral economy has managed to survive, mainly because creating friendship and loyalty became the main features. If Hirschman is right about the formula of a successful moral economy – namely that it is loyalty that enables voice and keeps exit at bay – then the *txoko* can serve as a prime example. As we have seen, loyalty is created through commensality, an intersubjective form of communication in which the end product (food and drink) is consumed collectively. Almost by definition and design it renders instrumental mean-ends rationality and communication meaningless – a key argument for the *txoko*'s success. Its main purpose is indeed not to care for immediate needs and survival – as indeed the *baserria* and the *cofradía* have to – but it is exactly its opposite, the pleasure and joy created through the consumption of good food and drink that is the *txoko*'s main *raison d'être*.

Over the course of half a millennium the *baserria* and the *cofradía* and for almost 120 years the *txoko* have been very successful in adjusting to the circumstances and the environment they have found themselves in. As we have seen in the individual chapters devoted to the evolution of the three institutions, changes there have been plenty, particularly from the late nineteenth century onwards. Often the Basques' response to these changes have been reluctant, but we have to understand that such reluctance was based on the conviction that change made only sense if it led to long-term improvement and security of the whole group. In other words, there has indeed been a collective dimension to responses to modernization challenges. This means that the individuals and social groups involved were not mere dupes of objective social structures. Instead, they were to some extent the makers of their own fortune. In this context the rhetoric of egalitarianism has indeed been a major tool, not just as a kind of gut reaction to modern challenges but as a moral force, a rallying call around which plebeian culture could gather and gain momentum. Such rhetoric helped people make history, even if that kind of history-making rarely made it into the annals or the history books. To sum up the argument, reluctant modernization is a hybrid form that has helped to mediate and negotiate between traditional and modern forms of life. It is a specific – or shall we better say, adequate – expression of the collective-subjective dimensions of plebeian culture and moral economy that some of the participants in the debates about the origins of Basque nationalism and the allegedly forgotten social inequality to which I referred in the Introduction rarely address and discuss. That individuals and groups can make and indeed have made history is the central message of this study. That they have made history under the peculiar circumstances and in a specific environment is the second part of the message. In doing so they have found their own answer – an attitude that can be described as being reluctant to modernize and taking on the peculiar institutionalized form of exit, voice or loyalty. The very fact that two of the three institutions have not survived should not be taken as a sign of failure. As a matter of fact, some traditional elements of both institutions have actually survived, although not in a form originally anticipated by their principle past protagonists.

Taking a closer look at how *fiestas* are organized in the Basque Country nowadays, any observer must be struck by the hybrid or fusion forms of some of these *fiestas*. A wonderful illustration of such fusion or hybrid form – or, as Claude Lévi-Strauss would say, *bricolage* form – is the annual celebration of the *fiestas de calvarios* in Mutriku, Gipuzkoa. Taking place for three consecutive days in early September, the fiesta is an ideal example of mixing the traditional with the modern, the rural with the semi-urban, the *baserria* culture with the *cofradía* and the life of the sea and the urban form of socializing as it persists and continues to survive in the *txoko*.

The *fiesta* starts usually with a mass in the local church that is situated in the rural environment of the seaside town, half-way up the mountain *Arno*, a 600-metre-high mountain that rises behind the town and forms part of its rural hinterland. The church and the church *plaza*, although situated in a rural environment, were built and financed by the local *cofradía* to celebrate mass for the fishermen. The wooden ship model that hangs from the church ceiling is still a sign of the link with the sea.

After mass in the morning, which is not visited by everyone – the younger generation rarely goes to mass these days – the people gather outside the *plaza* overlooking the surrounding rural pastures and the entire eastern Cantabrian coast up to France. The people present are mainly locals from Mutriku and its rural hinterland, the sons and daughters of former local *baserriak* and *cofradías*, now working in most cases somewhere else. Most of these people have been brought up together and they return now for the *fiesta* to celebrate with their *cuadrilla* and later on in their *txoko*. After a round of *txakoli* and some *pintxos* and after having watched some rural sports, everybody watches the soap-box race which follows the *txakoli* and *pintxos* and in which friends or sometimes entire *cuadrillas* race down the steep road from the small *calvarios* church to the main church and the *plaza* in town. Most people will now have descended into town, awaiting and greeting the soap box cars as they arrive. Another reception follows – it is lunch by now – and the *fiesta* continues with various entertainments until the next morning.

The second day takes place in the town and is again a celebration of the town people, most of them having some family connection to members of the *cofradía* or the various *baserriak* and their *casa en la calle*; they are further joined and supported by the various *cuadrillas* and other social, cultural and sometimes professional organizations and bodies. The day reaches a celebratory peak in the evening by a carnival-like procession through the town, starting at the lower *plaza*, the original place where the church was once located. (The actual grounds have been used for a market after the ground proved to be too unstable for a high-rise church building.) For dinner almost everyone goes with his or her *cuadrilla* to the *txoko* and eats there.

The third day consists of bull-running in the streets and in the port, followed by a boat procession where a plastic pig is shipped around the interior harbour. The highlight of this day is again a collective feast of *marmitako* in the various port facilities. *Marmitako* is a stew consisting of *bonito* (white tuna) and potatoes and is eaten by the *cuadrillas* during the last day of the *fiestas de calvarios*. It symbolizes as nothing else the fusion of rural, sea and urban forms of life – a hybrid or *bricolage* celebration of plebeian culture, moral economy, past and present, traditional and modern life indeed. To argue that such traditions are entirely invented, or are just militant expressions of a heroic past and ideology that has not really died, are mistaken and are missing the point: namely that, as Marx has pointed out, history can indeed be made – just not always under the circumstances chosen.

Glossary of Basque and Spanish Terms

abertzale: Basque patriot
agotes (pl.): excluded minority mainly in Navarre (lit. a native of the valley of Baztán in Navarre)
ahuntz: goat
aita: father
aitzur: hoe
aizkora: axe
alde: zone, part, district
ama: mother (in Spanish: housewife)
anteiglesias: small rural community
antxoa: anchovies
aperitivo: aperitif
ardi: sheep
armador: facilitator, financier, owner
arrain: fish
arrantzale: fisherman
arrastre (see also *pesca de arrastre*): trawling
artesanal: traditional (fishing)
artzain: shepherd
asamblea: meeting, official gathering
astillero: wharf, ship-building facility with launch pad
atalaya: watchtower
atalayero: guard, watchman
auzo: small rural settlement, nucleus or neighbourhood
auzorik hurrena: assistance from the immediate rural neighbour (*auzo*: neighbourhood; *hurrena*: nearest, immediate)
bacalao, *bacallu*: cod
bahia: bay
ballenero: whaler

barco: ship, vessel
barco de arrastre: trawler
barrio: neighbourhood, quarter
baserri, *baserriak* (pl): farm, farmstead
baserritarra: farm person, somebody who grew up in a rural environment
baso: forest
baso mojonauek: specific use of the commons
batzoki: bar of the Basque Nationalist Party (PNV/EAJ)
besugo: red bream
bildots: lamb
bisita: visit from next door rural neighbour in time of crisis or emergency
bodega: bar, wine cellar
bonito: white tuna
borda: mountain shelter, hut
cabela: small boat or vessel
caja: fund (lit. a box)
caja de ahorros: credit union, savings bank
cajetín: cash or deposit box
capitán: captain
capellán: religious affairs person, middleman between brotherhood and church/priest
carlista: supporter of the Carlist (traditional Basque) cause
carnaval: carnival
carta puebla: titles of town, foundation charter
casa de contratación: chamber, house of trade
casa en la calle: townhouse
casa solar: rural farmhouse
casa torre: protected farmhouse usually in shape of a large tower
casco viejo: old part of town
caserío (see also *baserri*): farm, farmstead
caya (see also *kai*): dock, pier
cebo vivo: live bait
chalupa: launch, small boat, skiff

chica: female helping hand (lit: young girl)
chiquiteo, *txikiteo* (see also *poteo*): bar rounds, pub-crawl
cocina vasca: Basque cuisine
codo: elbow, arm's length
cofradía (see also *kofradi*): brotherhood, confraternity, guild
cofradía de mareantes, *cofradía de pescadores*: brotherhood of fishermen
compañía: company
consulado: consulate
contador, *contra-contador*: accountant
contestador, *contra-contestador*: auctioneer, accountant
cordial (see also *cofradía* and *kofradi*): brotherhood
cordero: lamb
costera, *kostera* (see also *pesca de bajura* or *pesca litoral*): coastal fishing
cuadrilla, *kuadrila*: group of friends, clique, team, gang, squad
días de casa (see also *etxe egunek*): days at home
dueño: owner of ship or vessel
eguin: mansion house
ensanches: urban development zones, parts of the city
Estudios Vascos: Basque Studies
etxe: house
etxejabeak: small independent class of farmers (lit: house possessors)
etxekoak: occupiers of a house or farmstead, family members
etxekoandre: woman or lady of the household
etxekojaun: master of the house
etxe egunak (see also *días de casa*): days at home
Euskadi: Basque Country
Euskal Herria: Basque Country
familije: extended or co-opted part of the family
ferrería: iron works and metal factory
fiesta: celebration, big party
fueros: historic rights
galea: specific type of small boat
galera: galley
gaztandegia: collective for milk and cheese production
goitala: small boat or vessel

gremium (lat.): gathering, small assembly
grumete: helping hand, apprentice, cabin boy
guarda: watchman, security
Hegoalde: Spanish part of the Basque Country (lit. south)
hermandad: brotherhood, confraternity
herriko taberna: bar for radical patriots
hidalgia, hidalguía: nobility
hidalgo: nobleman
idi: ox
Iparralde: French part of the Basque Country (lit. north)
inauta (see also *partija*): share
itsaso, itxaso: sea
jaun: master
jauregi: mansion house, spacious home
junta: gremium, board
junta directiva: board of directors
kai (see also *caya*): dock, pier
kale: street
kaletarra: street-wise person
kofradi (sea also *cofradía*): brotherhood, confraternity, guild
korta: type of dispersed rural settlement
kostalde: coast, coastline
labrador: milk farmer, farm labourer
la (calle) de arriba: the upper street
la (calle) de enmedio: the middle street
la (calle) de abajo: the lower street
lan: work
lana: wool
latifundio: land ownership or estate based on huge land holdings
lehenbiziko atea: next-door neighbour visit in rural environment (lit. *lehenbiziko*: first)
loije: port tavern, usually close to the embarking/disembarking pier
maestro, maestro de pinaza: owner of a ship or vessel
maizterrak: self-sufficient tenant farmers
manta: share

marinero: mariner, sailor
matxinada: disturbances in the seventeenth and eighteenth centuries, mainly in the coastal areas of Bizkaia and Gipuzkoa
mayordomo: caretaker, president, steward or executive head of the brotherhood
merluza: hake
minifundio: type of land holding based on small and fragmented land
monte mayor: overall gain or income from sale
monte menor (sometimes also referred to as *reparto*, *mareaje de Santa Clara* or *soldato de San Telmo*): net income from sale after all expenses have been covered
motora: boat or small vessel with a motor
muchacho: helping hand on deck
muelle: pier
nagusia: master or upper class
nekazari: peasant farmer
nueva cocina vasca: new Basque cuisine
ordenanzas: statutes
oveja: sheep
partija: share
patrón: patron, owner
pelota: Basque ball game
pesca: fishing
pesca bajura, *pesca litoral* (see also *costera*): coastal fishing
pesca de altura: high sea fishing
pesca de arrastre: trawling
pesca de gran altura: deep sea fishing
pescado: fish
pescador: fisherman
plaza de toros: bullfighting arena
pósito: fund, mutual society
poteo (see also *chiquiteo* and *txititeo*): drinking session, bar rounds, pub crawl
real sociedad: royal society
regata: rowing competition

remero: rower, fisherman
revolución de sal: urban riots in Bilbao in the sixteenth century
sagardo: cider
sagardotegi (see also *sidrería*): cider house
salazonero: fish factory owner
sardinera: female sardine worker, small fishmonger (female)
segail: small goat
semana grande: literally the 'big week'; main fiesta in San Sebastián
señero, *señarelo*: signalman
señorío: reign, province
sepultura: church burial ground (lit. burial)
sidrería (see also *sagardotegi*): cider house
siesta: afternoon rest
sociedad gastronómica (see also *txoko*): gastronomic society, cooking society
sociedad popular: popular society
Sociedad Vascongada: Royal Basque Society
taberna: tavern
tambor: director of a marching or brass band (lit. drum)
tamborrada: event with a marching or brass band as its main attraction
tertulia: gathering that includes a discussion of the arts, aspects of philosophy, etc.
Terranova: Newfoundland
tostarteko: rower, fisherman, crew member
tripulación: crew
tripulantes: members of a crew
txakoli: white wine from Getaria
txakur: dog
txalupa (see also *chalupa*): launch, small boat
txerri puskak: sharing of pig after slaughter (lit. pieces of pork)
txo: apprentice, youngest member of the crew
txoko (see also *sociedad gastronómica*): gastronomic society, cooking society, (lit. corner)
universidades: isolated rural communities forming an alliance
vaca: cow

valle: valley
vecindad: neighbourhood
ventador (sometimes also *cantador*): auctioneer
villas ribereñas: towns located at the mouth of a river
zezen: bull

Bibliography

Agirreazkuenaga Zigorraga, J. (ed) (1995), *Los Vascos – Gran Atlas Histórico de Euskal Herria*, Bilbao: Lur Argitaletxea

Aguirre Franco, R. (1983), *Las sociedades populares*, San Sebastián: Caja de Guipuzkoa

Aguirre Franco, R. (2006), *Las sociedades populares, Donostia 1870–2005*, San Sebastián: Hiria

Alberdi Lonbide, X. 'La Cofradía de Mareantes de San Pedro en la Historia Pesquera de Motrico' (unpublished manuscript, undated)

Alonso Cespedes, M. (1996), *El caso de los txokos vascos: sociología de la fratria informal*, Bilbao: Tesina Sociológica, Deusto (unpublished)

Anton Idroquilis, P. (1994), *Comer en sociedad*, Vitoria-Gasteiz: Diputación Foral de Alava

Apraiz, J. and Astui, A. (1987), 'La pesca en Euskalerria. La pesca de litoral', in: *Itsasoa* Vol. 2, 119–220

Apraiz, J. and Astui, A. (1989), 'La pesca en Euskalerria. La pesca de bajura', in: *Itsasoa* Vol. 4, 74–148

Aranzadi, J. (2000), *Milenarismo vasco – Edad de oro, etnia y nativismo*, Madrid: Taurus

Aranzadi, J. (2001), *El Escudo de Arquíloco (Vol. I & II)*, Madrid: Antonio Machado Libros

Arpal, J. (1979), *La sociedad tradicional en el País Vasco*, San Sebastián: Aramburu

Arpal, J. (1982), *Educación y sociedad en el País Vasco*, San Sebastián: Txertoa

Arpal, J. (1985), 'Solidaridades elementales y organizaciones colectivas en el País Vasco (cuadrillas, txokos, asociaciones)', in: Pierre Bidart (ed.) *Processus socieaux: ideologies et practiques culturelles dans la societé basque*, Bayona: Maubec

Arrieta, L. (1996), *Mutriku – Una aproximación a nuestra historia*, Mutriku, Gipuzkoa: Mutrikuko Udala

Astorkiza, K. and Del Valle, I. (1998), 'Fisheries Policy and the Cofradías in the Basque Country: The Case of Albacore and Anchovy', Pamplona: *Public University of Navarre Working Papers*

Azurmendi, J. (1995), *Los españoles y los euskaldunes*, Hondarribia: Argitaletxe Hiru

Azurmendi, M. (1993), *Nombrar, Embrujar: Para una historia del sometimiento de la cultura oral en el País Vasco*, Irun: Alberdania

Barandiaran, J. M. (1925), 'Contribución al estudio de la casa rural y de los establecimientos humanos', in: *Anuario de la Sociedad de Eusko Folklore*, Gasteiz: Eusko-Ikaskuntza, 1–67

Baroja, J. C. (1944/1986), *De la vida rural vasca*, San Sebastián: Editorial Txertoa

Baroja, J. C. (1985), *Los vascos y el mar*, San Sebastián: Editorial Txertoa

Baroja, J. C. (1986), *Introducción a la historia social y económica del pueblo vasco*, San Sebastián: Editorial Txertoa

Baroja, J. C. (1990), *Los vascos*, Madrid: Ediciones Istmo

Baroja, J. C. (1998), *Ser o no ser vasco*, Madrid: Espasa

Baroja, J. C. (2003), *El laberinto vasco* (1977–88), Madrid: Caro Raggio

Barruso Barés, P. et al. (eds) (2004a), *Historia del País Vasco: Edad Media (Siglos V–XV)*, San Sebastián: Hiria

Barruso Barés, P. et al. (eds) (2004b), *Historia del País Vasco: Edad Moderna (Siglos XVI–XVIII)*, San Sebastián: Hiria

Barruso Barés, P. et al (eds) (2005), *Historia del País Vasco: Edad Contemporánea (Siglos XIX–XX)*, San Sebastián: Hiria

Basterrechea, F. (1928), 'Función de las cofradías y su evolución necesaria', in: *Eusko Ikaskuntza*, Donostia: Eusko-Ikaskuntza, 313–339

Beltza (1976), *El nacionalismo vasco*, San Sebastián: Txertoa

Beltza (1976a), *Nacionalismo vasco y clases sociales*, San Sebastián: Txertoa

Bidart, Pierre (2001), *La singularité basque*, Paris: Presses Universitaire de France

Bikandi, J. J. (1989), 'Aspectos sociales de la actividad pesquera. Ciclos laborales y Compañías', in: *Itsasoa* Vol. 4, 149–174

Braudel, F. (1972), *The Mediterranean and the Mediterranean World in the Age of Philip II* (2 Vols), New York: Harper and Row

Burca Isusi, J. M. (1987), *Traditional Basque Cooking*, Reno: University of Nevada Press

Camino, I. (1987), *Batzokis de Bizkaia*, Bilbao: Ediciones Alberdi

Cana, J. (1992), 'La sociabilidad en los estudios sobre la España contemporánea', in: *Historia Contemporánea*, No. 7, 183–205

Canal y Morell, Jordi (1993), 'El concepto de sociabilidad en la historiografia contemporánea (Francia, Italia y España)', in: *Siglo XIX*, No. 13, 5–25

Castells, L. and Luengo, F. (1988), 'El proceso de modernización de Guipuzcoa (1876–1920)', in: *Ekonomiaz* No. 9/10, 255–275

Ciriquiain-Gaiztarro, M. (1986), *Los puertos maritímos del País Vasco*, San Sebastián: Editorial Txertoa

Cross, J. M. (2001), 'Teoría y política en la antropología de Europa y el marco de investigaciones vascas', in: *Ankulegi* No. 5, 57–61

Cunliffe, B. (2001), *Facing the Ocean – The Atlantic and its Peoples*, Oxford: Oxford University Press

Delgado Cendagortagalarza, A. (1998), *Bermeo en el siglo XX. Política y conflicto en un municipio pesquero vizcaino (1912–1955)*, Zarautz: Colección Landidetzean

Departamento de Cultura de la Diputación Foral de Bizkaia (ed.) (1992), *Lekeitio*, Bilbao: Diputación Foral de Bizkaia

Douglass, W. A. (1975), *Echalar and Murelága – Opportunity and Rural Exodus in Two Spanish Basque Villages*, Houndmills: Macmillan

Douglass, W. A. (2003), *Muerte en Murelága*, Zarautz: Alga

Douglass, W. A. et al. (eds) (1999), *Basque Cultural Studies*, Reno, NV: University of Nevada Press

Douglass, W. and Zulaika, J. (2007), *Basque Culture: Anthropological Perspectives*, Reno, NV: Center for Basque Studies

Du Jourdin, M. M. (1993), *Europa und das Meer*, Munich: C. H. Beck

Durkheim, E. (1893/1984), *The Division of Labour in Society*, London: Macmillan

Egin Monografias (ed.) (1981), *Txokos y Sociedades*, Hernani: Egin Monografias

Elzo, J. (ed.) (2002), *Los valores de los vascos y navarros ante el nuevo milenio*, Bilbao: Universidad de Deusto

Enriquez Fernandez, J. C. (1994), 'El pensamiento agrario durante la Ilustración Vasca', in: Instituto Vasco de Estudios Rurales (ed.) *Pensamiento agrario vasco*, Bilbao: Universidad del País Vasco, 11–14

Erkoreka, A. (2003), *Etnografía de Bermeo*, Bilbao: Doniene

Erkoreka, J. I. (1991), *Análisis Histórico-Institucional de las Cofradías de Mareantes del País Vasco*, Vitoria: Gobierno Vasco

Erkoreka, J. I. (1991a), 'Aproximación histórica al estudio de las relaciones interinstitucionales entre las cofradías de mareantes y los municipios costeros vascos (La Junta Pescadora de Elantxobe)', in: *Bermeo*, No. 8, 171–223

Erkoreka, J. I. (1993), *Estudio Histórico de la Cofradía de Mareantes de Portugalete*, Bilbao: Ayuntamiento de Portugalete

Erkoreka, J. I. and Salmeron Murgiondo, G. (1998), *Itsas Arrantza*, San Sebastián: Diputación Foral de Gipuzkoa

Etxezarreta, M. (1977), *El caserío vasco*, Bilbao: Fundación C. de Iturriaga y M. de Dañobeitia

Eusko-Ikaskuntza (ed.) (1928), *Asamblea de pesca marítima vasca*, San Sebastián: Diputación de Guipuzkoa

Fernandez-Armesto, F. (2002), *Near a Thousand Tables – A History of Food*, New York: Free Press

Fernandez de Larrinoa, K. (ed.) (1998), *Sociedad rural, desarrollo y bienestar*, Vitoria: Universidad del País Vasco

Flandrin, J.-L., Montanari, M. and Sonnenfeld, A. (eds) (1999), *Food – A Culinary History*, New York: Penguin

Frobert, L. and Ferraton, C. (2003), *L'enquête inachevée – introduction à l'économie politique d'Albert O. Hirschman*, Paris: Presses Universitaires de France

Gandasegui Larrauri, J. M. (1936), *La industria pesquera en Vizcaya*, Madrid: Sociedad para el progreso social

García de Cortázar, F. (2005), *Atlas de Historia de España*, Barcelona: Planeta

Garcia-Orellán, R. and Beobide Arburua, J. (2005), *Hombres de Terranova: La Pesca de Bacalao 1926–2004*, San Sebastián: Zabaltzen

Garmendia Larrañaga, J. (1979), *Gremios, oficios y cofradías en el País Vasco*, San Sebastián: Caja de Ahorros

Garmendia Larrañaga, J. and Pena Santiago, L.-P. (1982), *El mar de los vascos* (Vol. I & II), San Sebastián: Txertoa

Gogeascoechea, A. (1994), 'El romanticismo 1800–1876', in: Instituto Vasco de Estudios Rurales (ed.) *Pensamiento agrario vasco*, Bilbao: Universidad del País Vasco, 71–76

Gomez Uranga, M. (2003), *Basque Economy – From Industrialization to Globalization*, Reno (NV): Center for Basque Studies

Gracia Cárcamo, J. (1985), 'Los conflictos sociales en la cofradía de pescadores de Bermeo a través de sus ordenanzas', in: *Congreso de Estudios Históricos. Vizcaya en la Edad Media*, Donostia: 371–373

Gracia Cárcamo, J. (1985a), 'La fiesta y las prácticas religiosas de los pescadores bermeanos en la segunda mitad del siglo XVIII', in: *Ernaroa – Revista de Historia de Euskal Herria*, No. 1

Gracia Cárcamo, J. (1986), 'La fiesta y las prácticas religiosas de los pescadores bermeanos en la segunda mitad del siglo XVIII', in: *Ernaroa*, No. 2, 35–53

Gracia Cárcamo, J. (1992), 'La evolución de las actividades pesqueras y de la Cofradía Maritíma', in: *Lekeitio*, Bilbao: Diputación Foral de Bizkaia, 113–142

Gracia Cárcamo, J. et al. (1983), *Historia de la economía maritíma del País Vasco*, San Sebastián: Editorial Txertoa

Greenwood, D. J. (1976), *Unrewarding wealth: The commercialization and collapse of agriculture in a Spanish-Basque town*, New York: Cambridge University Press

Gusfield, J. R. (1967), 'Tradition and Modernity: Misplaced Polarities in the Study of Social Change', in: *The American Journal of Sociology*, Vol. 72, No. 4, 351–362

Haranburu Altuna, L. (2000), *Historia de la alimentación y de la cocina en el País Vasco*, San Sebastián: Hiria

Heiberg, M. (1989), *The Making of the Basque Nation*, Cambridge: Cambridge University Press

Hess, A. (1999), 'The "economy of morals" and its applications – an attempt to understand some central concepts in the work of Albert

O. Hirschman', in: *Review of International Political Economy*, Vol. 6, No. 3, 338–359

Hess, A. (2001), *Concepts of Social Stratification – European and American Models*, Houndsmills: Palgrave-Macmillan

Hess, A. (2007), 'Is it justified to speak of a Jesuit Work Ethic in the Basque Country? – Variations on a Weberian Theme', in: *Max Weber Studies*, Vol. 7, No. 1, 89–96

Hess, A. (2007), 'The Social Bonds of Cooking: Gastronomic Societies in the Basque Country', in: *Cultural Sociology* Vol. 1, No. 3, 383–407

Hirschman, A. O. (1970), *Exit, Voice, and Loyalty: Responses to Decline in Firms, Organizations, and States*, Cambridge, Mass.: Harvard University Press

Hirschman, A. O. (1977), *The Passions and the Interests: Political Arguments for Capitalism before its Triumph*, Princeton, N. J.: Princeton University Press

Hirschman, A. O. (1982), *Shifting Involvements: Private Interests and Public Action*, Princeton, N. J.: Princeton University Press

Hirschman, A. O. (1989), *Entwicklung, Markt und Moral*, München: Carl Hanser Verlag

Hirschman, A. O. (1991), *The Rhetoric of Reaction: Perversity, Futility, Jeopardy*, Cambridge, Mass.: Harvard University Press

Hirschman, A. O. (1998), *Crossing Boundaries – Selected Writings*, New York: Zone Books

Homobono, J. I. (1987), 'Comensabilidad y fiesta en el ambito arrantzale. San Martín de Bermeo,' in: *Bermeo*, No. 6, 301–392

Homobono, J. I. (1989), 'San Urbano de Gazkue, ermita, romeria y otras expresiones de religiosidad popular', in: *Cuadernos de Etnología y Etnografía de Navarra*, Vol. 11, No. 54, 407–425

Homobono, J. I. (1990), 'Fiesta, tradición e identidad local', in: *Cuadernos de Etnología y Etnografía de Navarra*, Vol. 12, No. 55, 43–58

Homobono, J. I. (1997), 'Fiestas e el ámbito arrantzale. Expresiones de sociabilidad e identidades colectivas', in: *Zainak*, No. 15, 61–100

Hussey, R. D. (1934), *The Caracas Company 1728–1784: A Study in the History of Spanish Monopolistic Trade*, Cambridge, Mass.: Harvard University Press

Imaz, J. M. (1944), *La industria pesquera en Guipuzcoa al final del Siglo XVI*, San Sebastián: Imp. Diputación de San Sebastián

Instituto Vasco de Estudios Rurales (ed.) (1994), *Pensamiento agrario vasco*, Bilbao: Universidad del País Vasco

Iturbe, J. A. and Letamendia, F. (2000), 'Cultura, política y gastronomía en el País Vasco', in: Francisco Letamendia and Christian Coulon (eds) *Cocinas del mundo – La política en la mesa*, Madrid: Editorial Fundamentos, 45–78

Juaristi, J. (1987), *El linaje de Aitor. La invención de la tradición vasca*, Madrid: Taurus

Kamen, H. (2002), *Spain's Road to Empire – The Making of a World Power 1492–1763*, London: Allen Lane-Penguin

Kurlanski, M. (1997), *Cod*, New York: Walker and Company

Kurlanski, M. (2002), *Salt*, London: Jonathan Cape

Lambert, P. and Schofield, P. (eds) (2004), *Making History: An introduction to the history and practices of a discipline*, Abingdon: Routledge

Larriñaga Rodríguez, C. (2005), 'El País Vasco durante la Restauración (1875–1902)', in: Barruso Barés, P. et al. (eds) (2005), *Historia del País Vasco. Edad Contemporánea (Siglos XIX–XX)*, San Sebastián: Hiria, 145–176

Llona, J. L. (2001), 'Las formas de comer de los vascos a lo largo de la historia, con atención especial al siglo XX', in: *Nuevos Extractos*, Bilbao: Real Sociedad Bascongada de los Amigos del País, 9–101

Luengo Teixidor F. (2001), *San Sebastián – La vida cotidiana de una ciudad*, San Sebastián: Editorial Txertoa

Luengo Teixidor, F. (2005), 'El primer tercio del siglo XX', in: Barruso Barés, P. et al. (eds) (2005), *Historia del País Vasco. Edad Contemporánea (Siglos XIX-XX)*, San Sebastián: Hiria, 177–235

Maiz Alcorta, J. A. (1993), *El sector pesquero vizcaino. 1800–1960. Análisis de la interacción de los elementos ambiental, extractivo y comercial en la pesquería*, Gasteiz: Gobierno Vasco

Martínez G. C. (1993), *Casa, Provincia, Rey*, Irun: Alberdania

Martínez, J. (1994), 'La vida rural vasca desde la antropología social', in: Instituto Vasco de Estudios Rurales (ed.) *Pensamiento agrario vasco*, Bilbao: Universidad del País Vasco, 283–326

Martínez, J. and Ramón Mauleón, J. (1994), 'Sociedad rural tradicional y crisis del caserío an los años 1950–60', in: Instituto Vasco de Estudios Rurales (ed.) *Pensamiento agrario vasco*, Bilbao: Universidad del País Vasco, 275–282

Martínez Montoya, J. (2002), *La identidad reconstruida: espacios y sociabilidades en la ruralidad alavesa*, Vitoria-Gasteiz: Servicio Central de Publicaciones del Gobierno Vasco

Mauleón Gómez, J. R. (1998), *Estrategias familiares y cambios productivos del caserío vasco*, Vitoria: Gobierno Vasco

Maza Vease, E. (1997), 'La horizontalidad de las solidaridades. El mutualismo en la España contemporánea', in: *Ayer*, No. 25

MacClancy, J. (2007), *Expressing Identities in the Basque Arena*, Oxford: James Currey

Meldolesi, L. (1995), *Discovering the Possible – The Surprising World of Albert O. Hirschman*, Notre Dame, Ind.: University of Notre Dame Press

Mennell, S. (1996), *All Manners of Food*, Urbana and Chicago, Ill.: University of Illinois Press

Merion, J. M. (1986), *La pesca desde prehistoria hasta nuestros dias*, Vitoria-Gasteiz: Gobierno Vasco

Moore, B. (1967), *Social Origins of Dictatorship and Democracy*, London: Penguin

Morales, A. A. (2004), 'Las Fuentes de la riqueza y la economía de Frontera', in: Morales, A. A et al. (eds) *Historia del País Vasco: Edad Moderna*, San Sebastián: Hiria, 163–211

Moraza Barea, A. (2000), *Estudio Histórico del Puerto de Ondarroa*, Vitoria: Gobierno Vasco

Nuñez, L. (1977), *Clases sociales en Euskadi*, San Sebastián: Txertoa

Olabarri, I. (1985), 'Tradiciones cooperativas vascas', in: Inchausti, J. *Euskal Herria. Historia y sociedad*, Donostia, Caja Laboral Popular, 298–307

Ortíz de Orruño Legarda, J. M. (2005), 'Crisis del Antiguo Régimen y Revolución Liberal (1793–1878)', in: Barruso Barés, P. et al. (eds) *Historia del País Vasco. Edad Contemporánea (Siglos XIX–XX)*, San Sebastián: Hiria, 17–77

Otazu, A. de (1986), *El 'igualitarismo' vasco: Mito y realidad*, San Sebastián: Editorial Txertoa

Otazu, A. de and Díaz de Durana, J. R. (2008), *El espíritu emprendedor de los vascos*, Madrid: Sílex

Ott, S. (1993), *The circle of mountains*, Reno, NV: University of Nevada Press

Pascual Fernández, J. (1997), 'Campesinos y pescadores: un problema de definición', in: *Zainak*, No. 15, 15–28

Pauly, D. and Maclean, J. (2003), *In a Perfect Ocean – The State of Fisheries and Ecosystems in the North Atlantic Ocean*, Washington D.C.: Island

Pérez-Agote, A. (1986), *La reproducción del nacionalismo. El caso vasco*, Madrid: Centro de Investigaciones Sociologícas

Pérez-Agote, A. (2006), *The Social Origins of Basque Nationalism*, Reno, Nev.: University of Nevada Press

Pérez-Mallaina, P. E. (1998), *Spain's men of the sea*, Baltimore: Johns Hopkins University Press

Ramón Mauleón, J. (1994a), 'Causas de la emigración rural en el País Vasco: las aportaciones de Greenwood y Douglass', in: Instituto Vasco de Estudios Rurales (ed.) *Pensamiento agrario vasco*, Bilbao: Universidad del País Vasco, 327–338

Ramón Mauleón, J. (1994b), 'Crisis del caserío vasco en los anos setenta y sus perspectivas futuras: Miren Etxezarreta', in: Instituto Vasco de Estudios Rurales (ed.) *Pensamiento agrario vasco*, Bilbao: Universidad del País Vasco, 339–350

Real Sociedad Bascongada de los Amigos del País (eds) (2001), *Las formas de comer de los vascos a lo largo de la historia*, Supplement 6

Rebora, G. (2001), *Culture of the Fork*, New York: Columbia University Press

Rivera Medina, A. M. (1997), *Estudio Histórico del Puerto de Bermeo*, Vitoria: Gobierno Vasco

Rodger, N. A. M. (2004), The Command of the Ocean: A Naval History of Britain *(1649–1815)*, London: Allen Lane-Penguin

Rubio-Ardanaz, J. A. (1994), *La Antropología marítima subdisciplina de la Antropología sociocultural*, Bilbao: Universidad de Deusto

Rubio-Ardanaz, J. A. (2006), *Lemanes, sardineras y pescadores: Realidades marítimas en perspectiva antropólogia*, Santurtzi: Editorial grafema

Rubio-Ardanaz. J. A. (ed.) (2003), *La Pesca y el Mar: Cambio Sociocultural y Economico* (*Zainak* Special Issue), San Sebastián: Eusko Ikaskuntza

Ruiz Olabuénaga, J. I. and Blanco, M. C. (1994), *La inmigración vasca*, Bilbao: Universidad de Deusto, Serie Ciencias Sociales

Sada, J. M. (1981), *Dos siglos de tamborada*, San Sebastián: Caja de Ahorros

Sada, J. M. and Hernandez T. (2001), *Sociedad Euskal Billera 1901–2001*, San Sebastián: Kutxa

Santana, A. and Otero, X. (1993), *Baserria*, San Sebastián: Diputación Foral de Gipuzkoa

Sesmero Cutanda, E. (1997), 'Aproximación a las relaciones intracomunitarias de los pescadores bermeanos a mediados del siglo XIX', in: *Zainak*, No. 15, 219–232

Spang, R. (2001), *The Invention of the Restaurant*, Cambridge, Mass.: Harvard University Press

Tannahill, R. (1988), *Food in History*, New York: Three Rivers Press

Thalamas Labandibar, J. (1935), *Aspectos de la vida social vasca. El campesino, el pescador, el obrero*, Zarautz: Itxaropena

Thompson, E. P. (1978), *The Poverty of Theory and other essays*, London: Merlin Press

Thompson, E. P. (1980), *Plebeische Kultur und moralische Ökonomie*, Frankfurt: Ullstein

Thompson, E. P. (1991), *Customs in Common*, London: Merlin Press

Tönnies, F. (1878/1955), *Community and Association*, London: Routledge

Totoricagüena, G. (2004), *Basque Diaspora – Migration and Transnational Identity*, Reno, Nev.: Center for Basque Studies

Toussaint-Samat, M. (1992), *History of Food*, Oxford: Blackwell

Ugalde, M. (2004), *Nueva Sintesis de la Historia del País Vasco*, San Sebastián: Txartalo

Untzi Museoa/Museo Naval (ed.) (1996), *Itsas Memoria – Revista de Estudios Maritímos del País Vasco*, No. 1 (Special Issue: Estado de la cuestión de los estudios maritímos en el País Vasco), San Sebastián: Diputación Foral de Gipuzkoa

Untzi Museoa/Museo Naval (ed.) (2000), *Itsas memoria – Revista de Estudios Maritímos del País Vasco*, No. 3 (Special Issue: La pesca en el País Vasco), San Sebastián: Diputación Foral de Gipuzkoa

Urrutikoetxea Lizarraga, J. (1992), *En una mesa y compania. Caserío y familia campesina en la crisis de la 'Sociedad Tradicional' (Irun 1766–1845)*, San Sebastián: Facultad de Filosofia y Letras, Universidad de Deusto

Urzainki Mikeleiz, A. (1994), 'Pensamiento social agrario en las ponencias y lecciones de los primeros congresos de estudios vascos', in: Instituto Vasco de Estudios Rurales (ed.) (1994), *Pensamiento agrario vasco*, Bilbao: Universidad del País Vasco, 227–240

Urzainqui, T. and De Olaizola, J. M. (1998), *La Navarra Marítima*, Pamplona: Pamiela Etxea

Van der Loo, H. and Van Reijen, W. (1992), *Modernisierung – Projekt und Paradox*, Munich: DTV

Watson, C. (2003), *Modern Basque History: 18th Century to the Present*, Reno, Nev.: Center for Basque Studies

Weber, Max (1922/1968), *Economy and Society*, New York: Bedminster Press

Weber, Max (ed. Gerth, H. H. and C. W. Mills) (1946), *From Max Weber*, New York: Oxford University Press

Wijck, Anke van (2000), *Basque Male Cooking Societies*, Boston University: MA dissertation (unpublished)

Zalbide, M. (1998), 'Normalización lingüística y escolaridad: un informe desde la sala de máquinas', in: *Revista Internacional de los Estudios Vascos*, Vol. 43, No. 2, 355–424

Zulaika, J. (1981), *Terranova – The Ethos and Luck of Deep-Sea Fishermen*, St. John's, Newfoundland: Institute of Social and Economic Research – Memorial University of Newfoundland

Zulaika, J. (1988), *Basque Violence – Metaphor and Sacrament*, Reno, Nev.: University of Nevada Press

Zulaika, J. (1996), *Del Cromañón al Carnaval*, Donostia: Erein

Index